The Jewelled Staircase

by Geshe Wangyal

The Jewelled Staircase

by Geshe Wangyal

Snow Lion Publications
Ithaca, New York USA

Snow Lion Publications
P.O. Box 6483
Ithaca, New York 14851
USA

Printed in USA

Library of Congress Catalogue Number 86-22071

ISBN 0–937938–38–6

Library of Congress Cataloging-in-Publication Data

  Thupten Wangyal.
    The jewelled staircase:

    Bibliography: p.
    1. Buddhism — Doctrines. I. Title.
  BQ4132.T48 1986   294.3'42   86-22071
  ISBN 0-937938-38-6

Table of Contents

Acknowledgements

The late venerable Geshe Wangyal, translator and adapter of the various Tibetan texts that make up the chapters of this book, did not have the time to write these acknowledgements before his death in 1983 and thus I have undertaken to do so in his stead. In 1958 Geshe-la established Labsum Shedrub Ling, Tibetan Buddhist Learning Center (formerly Lamaist Buddhist Monastery of America), which brought people together to work on projects such as this book. In his first two books Geshe-la used this opportunity to thank those many people for their kind help and this tradition is continued here.

Although it has been over three years since Geshe-la died, those who helped him continue to do so. I would like to thank them all for their continued support, and especially mention some here.

First and foremost, I am deeply grateful to His Holiness the Fourteenth Dalai Lama for his compassionate spiritual guidance. His deep understanding of Geshe-la's aims has assured Geshe-la's work of an unbroken continuity. May His Holiness live for a long time in good health to assure that Buddha's teachings flourish.

I express my profound gratitude to my spiritual teacher,

7

Venerable Geshe Wangyal, for his many years of selfless and tirelessly patient efforts to produce in me some understanding of these and other precious teachings. His inspiring example opened my eyes to see the possibilities of being human. Through his great love and nurturing he showed me how to care for others. Having seen his wisdom at work, I know that it is possible to act in a correct way effectively to help others.

I would be remiss if in the beginning I did not mention two of Geshe-la's oldest patrons, the late Mr. Chester Carlson and his deeply religious wife, Mrs. Dorris Carlson, whose love and support for Geshe-la's work we are always striving to repay. I also cannot forget the kind assistance of Mr. and Mrs. C.T. Shen.

I must also mention here the late Alice Scudder Rayburn and the late Elsy Becherer both of whom not only helped to edit this book but bequeathed a portion of their estates to assure the promotion and extension of Geshe-la's work.

Geshe-la's dreams are all coming into reality through the continued loving-kindness and generosity of his patrons, students, and friends. I am profoundly grateful to Buff and Johnnie Chace for their great support, close friendship, and deep commitment during this time of transition. I will never be able to forget as well all the kind assistance of Sarah and Chip Lukas, given with such tireless loyalty and deep affection. I cannot mention everyone here, but I also want to thank Joel and April McCleary, Philip and Natalie Hauptman, and David and Vikki Urubshurow for their enthusiastic support, helpful advice, and valued friendship.

I deeply appreciate the efforts of those who were so helpful in preparing the final manuscript: Chip Lukas for his poetic composition and editorial skills, and Anne Klein and Elizabeth Napper for their invaluable editorial assistance and constant enthusiasm for Geshe-la's work.

I am especially thankful to my parents, Mr. and Mrs. Eric Cutler, who have always given me an over-abundance of love and support, and who through the years have come to be kind supporters of this work. And I am grateful to my wife Diana for working together with me in continuing Geshe-la's work.

Finally, I would like to express my thoughts of appreciation to Sidney and Yvonne Piburn, Jeffrey and Christine Cox, and Gabriel and Patricia Aiello, of Snow Lion Publications, for their much needed patience, advice, and keen interest in making Buddha's teachings available to Western readers.

Joshua Cutler
Washington, New Jersey

Preface

The late venerable Geshe Wangyal chose the selections presented in this book because he considered them essential topics for new Buddhists of Western countries to understand. He intended this book to provide a firm basis for understanding Buddha's teaching, especially when read along with his previous two books, the *Door of Liberation* and the *Prince Who Became a Cuckoo: A Tale of Liberation*. As such, this book reflects his main goal in teaching Americans over the twenty-eight years that he lived in the United States.

All the chapters are translations and adaptions of traditional presentations of the materials by authors well-known especially to the monk-scholars of Gomang College of Drebung Monastic University. Even the chapter that was written in Tibetan by the author himself, the "Precious Human Life", was derived from works of other Tibetan scholars. The author translated all the chapters into English and then adapted the original presentations slightly in order to clarify the meaning of the topics for someone who did not have the background of a Tibetan scholar. The chapters were then edited by Geshe Wangyal's students, myself being responsible for final editorial decisions.

The various chapters are arranged in an order that is consistent with the genre of texts known as the "stages of the path" (*lam rim*) literature. The particular "stages of the path" text that was chosen is presented as the final chapter, the "Foundation of All Excellence". Relevant portions of this text are given in italics at the beginning of each chapter, providing a kind of outline for the chapters.

Transliteration of Tibetan in parentheses is done in accordance with a system devised by Turrell Wylie; see "A Standard System of Tibetan Transcription", *Harvard Journal of Asiatic Studies*, Vol. 22, 1959, pp. 261-7. The names of Tibetan orders and authors are given according to Jeffrey Hopkins' system of "essay phonetics" for the sake of easy pronunciation; see his *Meditation on Emptiness* (London: Wisdom Publications, 1983), pp. 19-22. Also for the sake of easy pronunciation, the names of Indian scholars and systems are spelled in the body of the text with ch, sh, and ṣh, as opposed to the usual c, ś, and ṣ, although standard transliteration is followed for parenthetical material.

Introduction

I bow down to my kind root lamas, source of the teaching's treasures.

The author of this book, Geshe Wangyal, passed away on January 30, 1983 at the age of eighty-one. Geshe-la had profound insight into Buddha's teaching, and through his great compassion was the unexcelled teacher to many people, myself included. He manifested this knowledge in his everyday life and that life itself serves as a great inspiration to those who aspire to practice Buddha's teaching.

Were I to write this introduction according to Tibetan Buddhist tradition, it would be most appropriate to set forth Geshe-la's biography in order to show that he was qualified to translate and edit the teachings in this book. That biography, however, is so rich and varied that it would be a book unto itself. Therefore, although Geshe-la had a deep understanding of all Buddha's teachings, I will illustrate his knowledge of just one teaching by choosing certain events in his life, as he recounted them to me. That teaching is on the awareness mindful of impermanence and death, one of the most fundamental mental trainings in Buddhist practice.

One might well wonder why I choose to explain Geshe-la's awareness mindful of death and impermanence over the many other knowledges that he mastered. Actually, I did not choose it. I once attended an interview of Geshe-la in which the interviewer asked what teaching was most important in Geshe-la's life. He chose the teaching on impermanence and death. Furthermore, Geshe-la told me many stories about his life, and he would often ask me to recount the number of times that he came close to death. He would always point out that these experiences helped to extend his life. Also, in choosing the various sections of this book, Geshe-la conspicuously left out the teachings on the awareness mindful of impermanence and death. Though Geshe-la declared the manuscript for this book "ready" well before his death, he put off adding the final touches, and he never did have the time to finish it. Therefore, it seems fitting that a presentation of Geshe-la's life from the viewpoint of his awareness mindful of death and impermanence should be the final addition to the teachings in this book, for his death itself brought out the importance of cultivating such an awareness.

Geshe-la dedicated his entire life to the practice of Buddha's teaching. Above all, he was a teacher. He said that from a young age he had great confidence in his knowledge and in his ability to instruct others and take responsibility for their lives. He himself lived in accordance with what he taught. Therefore, by looking at his life we can see a reflection of the teaching itself: by choosing to look at his life from the viewpoint of his awareness mindful of death and impermanence, we can see how the teaching on death and impermanence is fundamental to the Buddhist path. That it is fundamental is also clear from the scriptures themselves. The mental training in the awareness mindful of death and impermanence is the first and thereby most basic mental training set forth in the "stages of the path" (*lam rim*) literature for those who would enter into the practices of the Buddhist path. The "stages of the path" teachings have their origin in Buddha's Perfection of Wisdom sutras.

They present the path as a gradual process of transformation for one practitioner, beginning with the mental trainings for a being of small capacity, proceeding to the mental
trainings for a being of middling capacity, and ending with
the mental trainings for a being of great capacity. The
awareness mindful of death and impermanence is the first
mental training of a being of small capacity and hence is
shared also by beings of middling and great capacity. Thus,
it is the basis for the production of all of the realizations on
the Buddhist path. In his *Door of Liberation*, Geshe-la translated the following teaching of the great Ḡa-dam-ɓa (*bka'
gdams pa*) geshe, Ɓo-ḍo-wa (*po to ba*), from *Precepts Collected from Here and There (bka' gdams thor bu)*, a collection
of Ḡa-dam-ɓa teachings:[1]

> Geshe Ɓo-ḍo-wa was asked by a lay practitioner
> (*upāsikā*), "To actually practice the Dharma
> [Teaching], what is most important?"
>
> "The most important thing is the meditation of
> impermanence. Meditate on impermanence, the
> imminence of death; it will cause you to begin prac-
> ticing the Dharma. This will create conditions im-
> pelling you to do virtuous work, which will then
> assist you in realizing the equality of all things in
> their nature of existence."
>
> "Meditation on impermanence will also cause
> you to decide to renounce the enjoyments of this
> life, which will create the conditions for ridding
> yourself of all worldly desire, and thus assist you to
> enter the path of nirvana."
>
> "When you have meditated on impermanence
> and have gained some understanding, you will seek
> the Dharma. This will create the conditions for the
> achievement of Dharma and thus assist in its final
> accomplishment."
>
> "Meditating on impermanence and finding some
> understanding of it will cause you to commence the
> efforts of armor, which will create the conditions for

commencing the effort of religious practice. This
will assist you in commencing effort to the stage of
nonreturning."

From the time I met Geshe-la in 1970 when he was
sixty-nine years old, he constantly talked about his imminent death. This was very disquieting to me as a new
student, but Geshe-la's older students reassured me that he
had been doing so from as early as any of his American
students could remember. He did not just talk about it, but
seemed convinced that he would die soon. When he retired
from employment as age sixty-two, he had refused his So-
cial Security check, thinking that he would not live long
enough to find it useful. It was certainly not his health that
led him to this decision, for he was still renovating houses at
age seventy-nine.

Where had this striking awareness mindful of his own
impermanence come from? To answer this question, we
must look into Geshe-la's life prior to coming to the United
States.

Geshe-la came to the United States in 1955 to serve as a
priest for a Kalmuck-Mongolian community that had been
relocated to New Jersey after World War Two. Geshe-la
was born in 1901 amongst the Kalmucks, who are Tibetan
Buddhists, in the region of Russia west of the Volga River
known as Astrakhan Province. The Kalmucks had settled
there in the early seventeenth century. Geshe-la was the
youngest of four children and had chosen at age six to enter
the monastery as a novice monk. Before he started his
formal studies he had shown a clear sign that he would be
an unusual student — he was able to recite in Tibetan the
prayer for taking refuge in the Three Jewels without having
previously heard or seen it.

Yet Geshe-la apparently had no such innate, clear realization with respect to death and impermanence at this early
age. This can be seen in Geshe-la's story of the death of one
of his uncles, which he would relate with great regret at his
own ignorance. At the time Geshe-la was nine years old.

This uncle, also a monk, was special to Geshe-la because he had taught him how to pronounce Tibetan. The uncle's pronunciation was unusually good, for, unlike most Kalmuck monks, he could pronounce the Tibetan letter "nga" correctly.

When a Kalmuck became very ill, the most common cure prescribed was to give the patient only hot boiled water, never any food. Thus when Geshe-la's uncle became terminally ill, he was allowed only boiled water. Early one morning the young Geshe-la and a friend were playing near the uncle's bed when the uncle asked for food. Geshe-la answered, "Oh uncle, you know that you can't have anything to eat," and did not give him food. Then the uncle appeared to fall asleep.

Geshe-la later noticed that the uncle was no longer in the bed and asked a relative what had happened to him. His relative quite bluntly told him that his uncle had died. Geshe-la remembered thinking, "Oh, so death is like that!", for he had not understood that his uncle actually had died when he appeared to fall to sleep.

When Geshe-la told this story he regretted that he did not know enough to give his uncle something to eat. He felt pity that he had refused his uncle in his moment of great need.

Though Kalmuck country was part of Russia, the Kalmucks were left mostly on their own by the Russian people. Those Russians who lived nearby tended to stay out of the Kalmuck area because the young Kalmuck men would rough up unwanted visitors who strayed too far into the center of their region.[2] The Russian Orthodox church did have enough influence to make sure that Buddhist temples looked more like Christian churches, and the Czar's government conscripted young Kalmuck men into the armed forces and attempted to control epidemics by inoculation. Aside from these infrequent intrusions, life in Kalmuck country was quite free of outside influence. This made life for the Kalmucks easier in some ways and more difficult in others. In particular, the lack of proper medical help made epidemics a regular occurrence in the summers.

Each summer one out of every three persons would die from disease. Geshe-la fell ill every year but no illness was as severe as the one he had at age eighteen. His older brother, Gunsang, who was also a monk and Geshe-la's teacher, was the first to come down with the disease, which consisted primarily of a very high fever. Gunsang became delirious and had hallucinations of the messengers of the Lord of Death coming to take him away. He then broke into constant song until the fever finally broke. About twenty days passed before he was completely cured. During this time Geshe-la's mother was infected by the illness. Shortly thereafter Geshe-la also became sick.

Geshe-la went into a coma for twenty-three days. His mouth became full of scabs and his only sustenance was drops of boiled water poured through a tube into his mouth. He was cared for at home. Though sick herself, his mother would clean out his mouth with her tongue. (Geshe-la often told this story to illustrate a mother's loving-kindness to her child, an important model in Buddhist teachings on developing compassion as a part of the process of generating the altruistic aspiration to highest enlightenment for the sake of all beings.) Soon after this, before he regained consciousness, Geshe-la's mother died.

Geshe-la came out of his coma by awakening from a dream in which his mother had placed some food under his pillow. He awoke saying, "Please give me the food that my mother put under the pillow." An uncle who was attending him was so surprised to hear Geshe-la talk that he thought that Geshe-la was showing his last signs of life.

Gunsang had been watching over his brother while he was in his coma and then supervised his recovery, which was almost as tortured as the illness itself. At first he was allowed only to drink boiled water. Then a piece of meat was boiled in twenty cups of liquid and the resultant soup — but not the meat — was given to him. The strength of this soup was increased gradually.

Geshe-la was so hungry that he tried hard to obtain something more substantial. After ten days he persuaded a friend to give him a piece of meat and immediately his condition worsened. Gunsang was furious and the doctor ordered him back on boiled water.

Fearing that Geshe-la would have a relapse, Gunsang had been very careful not to tell Geshe-la that their mother had died. But two weeks after coming out of his coma, a young niece blurted out the sad news. Just as Gunsang had feared, Geshe-la had another relapse, weeping uncontrollably. Even after his full recovery he wept deeply during a visit to his eldest brother.

Geshe-la remembered the great adversity of this illness as being an important factor in extending his life. He often remarked that the extended period without food had strengthened his body. However, he was also critical of the extreme method of cure, saying that going without food for such a long time saps the body of the strength needed to fight the illness. Geshe-la said that he had survived only through his great physical strength and will power. These two characteristics helped him to live a long life, but, as he often said, they were also indications that his death would not be easy.

When Geshe-la was twenty-one years old, he left Kalmuck country to continue his studies in Lhasa, Tibet, for Tibet was the holy country for the Kalmucks. Even the word, "Tibet", may have its origin in the Mongolian language. In Mongolian, the term "Tibot" means "central region", which Geshe-la said refers to Tibet as the center of Buddhist religion. Thus, to study there was a great privilege. Geshe-la's brother Gunsang cried for a whole week before Geshe-le left for Tibet. He was not crying over the loss of a brother, but was only overjoyed that his brother was going to study in the holy center of religion.

Geshe-la left Kalmuck country just after the end of the Bolshevik Revolution, a very turbulent and dangerous time. Many Kalmucks died in the fighting or of starvation.

Geshe-la's life was threatened more than once by revolutionaries and brigands. He also endured great hardships on the journey to Tibet, which was expected to take just four months, but lasted over one year. At the end of the trip, his caravan was near starvation. However, Geshe-la did not consider any of these instances as unusually close brushes with death, but rather to be just part of the difficult and harsh life in those countries.

When Geshe-la reached Tibet he entered the Gomang College of Drebung Monastic University in Lhasa. Traditionally, Gomang was where the monks from the Kalmuck and other Mongolian regions would continue the studies they had begun in their homelands. The Tibetan Buddhist course of philosophical study is founded on the treatises of the most renowned Indian commentators on Buddha's teaching. The method of education involves study of texts with a teacher, memorization, and debate that draws upon the content of the first two. The novice monk begins with the study of logic and then pursues five topics of study in the following order: 1) Collected Topics of Valid Cognition; 2) The Perfection of Wisdom (*prajñāpāramitā*); 3) Middle Way (*mādhyamika*); 4) Discipline (*vinaya*); and 5) Treasury of Manifest Knowledge (*abhidharmakośa*). At the end of the course of studies, which can take as long as thirty-five years, one is awarded the degree of "geshe" (*dge bshes*), literally, "spiritual teacher".

The Kalmuck students had a great advantage over the Tibetan students because they had already begun these philosophical studies in their home monasteries and would enter their course in Tibet by repeating the study of the Perfection of Wisdom. Geshe-la had excelled in his studies in his homeland and did not want to spend his time just repeating material that he had already learned very well. He made better use of his time by simultaneously studying the next topic of studies. Geshe-la thus made great effort, at times to the point of overstraining himself. This strenuous study in combination with a custom of consuming as many as fifty cups of very strong Tibetan tea every day was responsible for his next close brush with death.

During this time Geshe-la shared a room with a number of other monks, including the Kalmuck teacher, Geshe Chim-ba, who was renowned in Tibet for his deep insight into Buddha's teaching. Geshe-la was not Geshe Chim-ba's student, but was close to him because Geshe Chim-ba was from the first class to graduate from Kalmuck country's first school of Buddhist philosophical studies. One night Geshe-la arose from bed while still asleep and walked towards the open window. Fortunately, Geshe Chim-ba was awake and yelled loudly, waking him just before he walked out the window and fell to certain death a number of stories below.

This was not an unusual occurrence in the monasteries. The strain of rigorous study affected such a number of students that there was even a name for the result — "geshe disease". In Geshe-la's case it was a temporary ailment, for he never had another occurrence. Realizing that he was pushing himself too hard, Geshe-la found a better pace, though he did not abandon studying two topics at once.

Geshe-la continued his studies at Gomang until 1932 when he decided that he should return to his homeland to find the financial support that was necessary to obtain his geshe degree. The Kalmuck students in Tibet received financial support from family and friends back home. Before Geshe-la had left for Tibet, he had sold some of his family's livestock in the Russian market in nearby Volgograd (then called "Tsaritsen"). With the money he received, Geshe-la bought Russian embroideries, which were highly valued in Tibet. In addition, Geshe-la's brother, Gunsang, had sent more embroideries after Geshe-la had been in Tibet for a few years. Thereafter, no money came from Kalmuck country because of the severe Communist repression. However, the money which Geshe-la did have supplied his needs well until it became time to return home to obtain the money needed to make the required offerings for his degree.

Again the trip involved great hardship. This time the route home was by way of Peking, and Geshe-la's companions abandoned him on the way, leaving him to fend for himself, unable to speak any Chinese. In addition to this mental hardship, the physical conditions were very difficult. For example, Geshe-la once suffered frostbite sitting on the frozen deck of a merchant steamer. However, he eventually reached Peking and stayed there after some Buryat Mongol monks warned him of the severe repression of religion in Russia.

Although Geshe-la could not converse with anyone on the way to Peking, he did know two words: "Peking" and "Yung-ho-kung". The latter was a large Tibetan Buddhist monastery in Peking, and was the place where Geshe-la stayed. It also came very close to being his final resting place.

At Yung-ho-kung, Geshe-la shared a room with another monk. In the winter the rooms were very cold but the beds were heated by lighting a charcoal fire in a little compartment under the bed. The heat from this fire then circulated under the bed, making it quite comfortable to sleep in. However, the fire posed the danger of carbon monoxide fumes. This was obvious to Geshe-la but not so to his roommate. Geshe-la constantly argued with the man to keep a small window open at the top of the wall.

One night, Geshe-la was sound asleep when his roommate came in late. Without waking Geshe-la, he lit his fire, closed the small window, and fell asleep. Slowly the fumes started to affect the two sleeping monks. The roommate was conscious enough to realize that something was wrong and tried to get up. As he did so, he fell out of bed with a thunderous crash.

The walls between the monk's rooms were literally paper thin. Though it was late, three monks were still awake in the adjoining room. They heard the noise and rushed in, finding Geshe-la almost unconscious in his bed and the roommate struggling to his feet. They grabbed Geshe-la, dragged him out into the cold winter night, and laid him down upon the icy ground. This brought Geshe-la to his senses. His head was pounding and he felt very groggy. The cold became difficult to bear and he pleaded wth his rescuers to bring him back inside. But the three monks would not listen because they knew that only the cold fresh air would restore him. He lay like that for what seemed a long time until finally he was conscious enough to go back inside.

Geshe-la had been working in Peking on a research project that was sponsored by Western donors. His job was to compare different editions of the Tibetan collections of Buddha's word (*bka' 'gyur*) and of the treatises of Indian commentators (*bstan 'gyur*). He made a respectable monthly salary of thirty Chinese dollars. Therefore he was able to reward his rescuers with enough money to make them very pleased.

Geshe-la stayed in China until he had earned enough money to make offerings for his geshe degree, and in about 1936 he set out to return to Tibet via India. When he reached Calcutta, he was introduced to the great English statesman, scholar, and explorer, Sir Charles Bell. Geshe-la had acquired a working knowledge of the English language while in Peking, and was thus qualified to become Bell's translator. He accompanied Bell on a trip through China and Manchuria before returning to Tibet. Eventually Geshe-la received his geshe degree, but he never again resided within the monastery. Instead, he used his capital and many contacts to make money with which he assisted many poor scholars to obtain their geshe degrees, especially the Mongolians, who, like him, were cut off from support from home.

During the Second World War, Geshe-la would spend his summers in Tibet and his winters in India in a small hill station called Kalimpong, near Darjeeling. The trip from Tibet was a difficult ride on horseback down through Gangtok, Sikkhim. One time when Geshe-la was making this trip he had a particularly wild horse whom he had nicknamed "Nyom-ba" ("Crazy"). When Geshe-la dropped behind the caravan, this horse suddenly became uncontrollable and charged ahead in order to catch up to the others. The trail was a steep and winding switchback. Instead of following the trail, the horse went straight down the hill, cutting across the switchbacks and heading right for a precipice. Geshe-la quickly understood that he was not going to be able to bring his horse under control, and just as he was approaching the edge of the cliff, he jumped off, holding on to the long reins. He landed on his buttocks, bruising the tip of his spine. At the same time he yanked the horse around, saving the horse's life. Fortunately, the horse knew what Geshe-la was trying to do when he yanked him back. He had barely missed going over the huge cliff. With his great presence of mind, Geshe-la had again narrowly escaped death.

It was around this time, at age forty-five, that Geshe-la decided to ask Mok-jok Rimbochay, a famous reincarnate lama from Gomang Monastic College, to divine an estimation of how long he would live. Mok-jok Rimbochay was a very well-known teacher, who was also proficient at divination. Geshe-la had a firm belief in this lama's ability to see into the future for he had done so for Geshe-la one time previously. About four years after arriving in Tibet, Geshe-la ran into some misfortune and needed guidance. As previously mentioned, Geshe-la had brought with him to Tibet many Russian embroideries, and by gradually selling these off, he was able to finance his stay, as did most of the Kalmuck students at the monasteries. One day while he was praying at the monastic assembly, a Mongolian monk entered his room and stole the embroideries. The thief sold the goods at a shop on the outside of Lhasa, where one of Geshe-la's Kalmuck friends immediately noticed them. The friend informed the shopkeeper that the goods had been stolen and the shopkeeper was able to apprehend the thief.

The Drebung monastery magistrate (*zhal ngo*) banished

the thief after confiscating all his possessions, including those belonging to Geshe-la. He did not return these to Geshe-la, but, because he was from Geshe-la's monastic college, he did spare him the usual intense questioning as to how he had acquired such valuable possessions when the vast majority of the monks were so poor. Although Geshe-la had broken no rules, he could have had a very difficult time because the magistrate had great authoritarian power and Geshe-la was still a new monk. Still Geshe-la was left without material support very early in his studies.

Geshe-la could see no alternative to making a return trip to Russia, but he decided to first consult Mok-jok Rimbochay. At this early time he did not know Mok-jok Rimbochay personally and asked a friend to act as mediator. When the friend asked the lama whether it was auspicious for Geshe-la to make the trip home, the lama consulted his oracular dice.[3] After casting the dice, the lama asked Geshe-la's friend whether he had heard that any of Geshe-la's friends had come to Tibet. The friend replied, "If I had, I certainly would not be here!" The lama, however, felt certain that Geshe-la's friends had arrived in Tibet, but he decided not to say so directly at the risk of speaking a lie. Instead, he advised that Geshe-la should wait a while.

At the very moment that the lama was being consulted, travelers from Russia had arrived at the northern Tibetan border town of Chang-nak-chu-ka, bearing new embroideries for Geshe-la from his brother, Gunsang. Two months passed before the caravan arrived in Lhasa and Geshe-la's goods were delivered to him.

Geshe-la was quite certain that there was no conventional way that the lama could have known about the foreigners' arrival at the Tibetan border. The only explanation was that Mok-jok Rimbochay possessed clairvoyance. Thus, this event established Geshe-la's faith in Mok-jok Rimbochay's knowledge and set a firm foundation for his later question regarding the length of his life. Moreover, when the lama answered that question and predicted that Geshe-la would not live to be more than fifty years old, Geshe-la produced the strong faith required to follow the lama's advice. The lama instructed Geshe-la to enter a retreat and devote himself to his special deity (*lhag pa'i lha*), the female Bodhisattva, Tara, by performing certain rituals and making a strong effort to recite the "Prayer to the Twenty-One Emanations of Tara" and the Tara mantra.

Mok-jok Rimbochay assured Geshe-la that, if he followed his precept, he could get rid of the obstacle to his life. Therefore, Geshe-la asked his closest friend, Geshe Chö-nyen, a Kalmuck monk who had accompanied him from Russia, to bring him food each day, and went into retreat. He remained in prayer and meditation day and night for three weeks.

Geshe-la would later refer to this retreat as a major cause in extending his life. Another cause was the complete change in his attitude towards his own death. At this point he decided that he would not live much longer. The experience of coming so close to death those four times, combined with the prophecy of Mok-jok Rimbochay, seemed to have had their effect. Moreover, there was another immediate factor that made him doubt his longevity. His longtime association with the British in Tibet, stemming from his job as translator for Sir Charles Bell, brought him under the suspicions of the Tibetan government. He was always worried that he would be falsely accused .and arrested as a British spy.

Geshe Chö-nyen and he determined that it would be best to part now rather than suddenly at Geshe-la's death. Geshe-la also was concerned that Geshe Chö-nyen literally would die from worry if Geshe-la were to die first. They were very close to each other, "as if of the same mind," as Geshe-la said. They had not known each other well in Kalmuck country but had become very close on the trip to Tibet. When their caravan reached Ulan Bator in Outer Mongolia, Geshe Chö-nyen went to town with another monk from the caravan and got into trouble. The leader of the caravan wanted to banish them both but Geshe-la stood up for Geshe Chö-nyen, saying that the leader would have to banish Geshe-la himself as well. Thereafter, the two were fast friends.

Now Geshe Chö-nyen had an opportunity to serve the family of a government official in Amdo province. Geshe Chö-nyen — medical doctor as well as geshe — at one time had saved the official's life. It seemed like a much more secure situation. Geshe Chö-nyen was a good scholar in Buddhist philosophy but always had strong faith in Geshe-la's knowledge, though he had no opportunity to receive teachings from him. Therefore, before parting, Geshe Chö-nyen bowed down to Geshe-la, received a short teaching, and made sincere aspirational prayers to be reborn as Geshe-la's disciple. Geshe-la arranged for people who lived along the way to attend to Geshe Chö-nyen's needs. However, the preparations did not prove to be enough. On the way to take up his new position in Amdo province, Geshe Chö-nyen contracted a stomach ailment and, ironically, died.

In the years immediately following, Geshe-la continued to travel between Tibet and India, and to assist monks to receive their geshe degrees. Finally in 1950 he decided to stay in Tibet. He was considering the purchase of a hermitage when he received news that the Chinese, who already had entered Amdo province, had started to move towards Lhasa. He immediately left for Lhasa to pick up all his belongings, and then set out for India as quickly as possible. He waited there for four years to get his visa to come to the United States to serve the newly settled Kalmuck community which had been displaced to southern New Jersey after World War Two, and finally arrived in New York City on February 5, 1955.

From the relatively young age of forty-five, Geshe-la felt certain that his death was imminent. For him to part with such a dear friend at a time that most would consider early in life certainly indicates the depth of his decision about his own mortality. That he lived another thirty-six years beyond this age supports his assertion that his awareness of death was helpful to extending his lifespan. His description of how such an attitude extended his life was based in the teachings of the Ḡa-dam-ба lamas, an early lineage descended from the great Indian teacher, Atisha, who was an important figure in the second dissemination of Buddhism to Tibet in the eleventh century A.D. The lamas in this lineage taught that when one has attachment to attaining a certain worldly objective, its attainment will always elude one. But once one does not have such attachment to that objective, its attainment will come to one incidentally. In other words, once one is focused on spiritual objectives with the unselfish attitude of non-attachment, worldly attainments come as a kind of by-product. As Atisha himself stated in *Precepts Collected From Here and There*:[4]

> If you act according to the Dharma [Teaching] from the depths of your heart, both food and necessities will come naturally.

This teaching is true with regards to Geshe-la's lifespan. From age forty-five Geshe-la never thought that he would live long. He gave up any thought of staying and was always prepared to go. But this did not mean that he gave up doing anything. On the contrary, as stated in the teaching of Geshe Bo-ḍo-wa cited above, his awareness mindful of death impelled him in his practice, for the second half of his life was the most productive in terms of directly helping a greater number of people. After arriving in the United States, he worked to earn enough money to establish a monastery, Labsum Shedrub Ling, among the Kalmucks. He served as the monastery's head teacher until his death, guiding and inspiring many Americans into a correct understanding of Tibetan Buddhist teachings. Geshe-la also greatly aided the Tibetan monasteries in India with financial assistance as well as by sponsoring Tibetan monks' stays at his monastery. He was constantly focused on others' welfare, and it was clear that he had attained many good qualities that were a result of actualizing Buddha's teachings. It was as if these realizations had arisen from his basic awareness mindful of death and impermanence.

In addition to impelling Geshe-la to help others, his mindfulness of death seemed to give him a greater appreciation of and enthusiasm for life. He used a variety of methods to inspire this in his students. He loved to play chess and sometimes would spend whole days playing against his students. Whether he won or lost, he never got tired of the play, constantly teasing and joking with his opponent. In the spring and summer he would rise early in the morning and take a walk outside just to breathe in the fresh air and enjoy the new smells and sounds.

He approached any work with the same energy. He loved to build, working late into the night and rising again early the next morning. It was very difficult for his students to keep up with him, although they were many years younger. He was always initiating new projects to improve the monastery's facilities, and he both joined in and directed the work, for he enjoyed working and used manual labor as a teaching vehicle. He had the same approach to cooking. He always prepared the meals, with his students assisting and learning more than just how to cook. In the same loving way, he also enjoyed spending many hours at sewing clothes for his students and friends.

Geshe-la's awareness of the imminence of death did not make him dour and unpleasant to be around. On the contrary, he attracted students because it was clear that for Geshe-la life was never boring or too difficult to bear. He had an inquisitive mind that was eager to learn new things. For instance, he started to learn Russian when eighty years old, hoping that he could see his homeland once more before his death. He never got stuck in the same routine. Even when he repeated a reading for new students, he would explain the teachings as if he were being inspired by the material for the first time.

Geshe-la's awareness of death continued to develop after

he was forty-five years old. He used to say that in developing an awareness mindful of death, at first one is afraid of death, then one accepts death without fear, and finally one can die happily. As Geshe-la translated in his *Door of Liberation* from *Precepts Collected From Here and There*:[5]

> Geshe Pu-chung-wa (*phu chung ba*) said, "Though we have obtained the indispensable human body with its leisure and opportunity, we do not have the power to stay in it — we have to die. At the time of death, we cannot take with us any of the enjoyments or concepts of this life, just as a tree sheds all its leaves. At that time the measure of our knowledge, our strength, and the wisdom of our goals will be clear. When we face death happily and with joyful anticipation, we are wise, strong; our goals are noble, and we will enter death clear-headed. But if at that time the form of Yama [the Lord of Death] and the distinct sign of lower states of rebirth appear, our goals are foolish and we are without self-mastery."

Geshe-la would often say in his later years how he was happy to die. He seemed content with what he had accomplished in this life. It was not that he wanted to die, for his compassion for others kept him actively teaching until his last breath.

Thus, being happy to die does not mean that one wants to die. I remember the Dalai Lama's late senior tutor, Ling Rimbochay, making this point to Geshe-la when I accompanied Geshe-la on a visit to India in 1978. Geshe-la considered Ling Rimbochay to be one of his root lamas and had a very deep reverence for him. Geshe-la and he were about the same age, so I imagined that death's immediacy was a concern for both of them. Ling Rimbochay told the story of the death of one of their contemporaries who was also an important teacher and with whom Ling Rimbochay had talked a few months before his death. At that time, the man had expressed a wish to die, though he was not especially unwell. Ling Rimbochay seemed very disappointed in his attitude, especially when he told Geshe-la that the man died only a few months later. He pointedly said, "Death is not good!" At the end of the audience, he seemed to be supporting his point when he presented Geshe-la with a painting of White Tara encircled by other deities of long life and instructed Geshe-la to do the same Tara prayers and rituals that Mok-jok Rimbochay had told him to do, though not in a retreat.

Geshe-la never gave up his will to live. With it he made the suffering of old age seem quite bearable. But he never let his students think that old age was enjoyable and would often bemoan its hardships. On one such occasion I remember saying to Geshe-la that he was doing well and leading a comfortable life. He replied, "You think it's so easy. The only reason that I am still alive is because of my strong will!"

Yet, it was not a matter of simply giving up this will to live when Geshe-la did die. His students, myself included, would often ask him not to die, but to stay and teach. His reply would be, "If I had the power to stay, I would certainly do so. I do not want to die, but I do not have that power. When the Lord of Death comes for me, I have no choice but to go." In other words, when the merit that sustains one is exhausted, one must die. There is no choice at that time and the will to live will not carry one further.

Geshe-la often told a story of what he considered to be an ideal way to die. During the Bolshevik Revolution, the young Geshe-la had witnessed the death of one of the great teachers who was qualified to give teachings (*lung*) that transmitted the lineage from Buddha's time to the present, as well as initiations (*dbang*). He was about sixty-five years old, which at that time was considered quite old. This great teacher, called a "Bakshi" in the Kalmuck language, was visiting his nephew, who was the head teacher of Geshe-la's temple. Because of the revolution, such famous teachers had to keep moving from place to place in fear of their lives. As he was just about to leave Geshe-la's temple, he decided to visit the outhouse. He sent his nephew ahead, and went with his very loyal and kind attendant. The Bakshi took an unusually long time in the outhouse, causing his attendant to open the door to see what the delay was. He found the Bakshi with his sash untied and quickly helped him to retie it, for the Bakshi had recently had a cold and the attendant did not want him to get a chill.

As the Bakshi was walking back to his horse cart, he suddenly sat down upon the ground. The attendant called to Geshe-la and his friends to bring a rug to put under him, and sent someone to bring the nephew back. The Bakshi sat very quietly, breathing deeply. Four monks very carefully carried him on his rug into the temple. He did not die before his nephew's return but sat still, and seemed to be reciting mantras internally, his breath becoming less and less perceptible.

When the nephew returned, he immediately started to quietly recite aspirational prayers, tears streaming down his face. The Bakshi's outer signs of life disappeared, except for a very slight breath that he was using to recite mantras. In this way he died very peacefully.

Geshe-la would conclude this story by saying that he did not expect to have such an easy death, and that he was too strong-willed to go easily. In the end, the intense suffering of his terminal illness was extremely difficult to bear. But his death was in a sense easy in that he was well-prepared and in control. Certainly, his death was a confirmation of the depth of his awareness mindful of death and impermanence.

Geshe-la's preparedness was such that he even understood well that his time to die was approaching. This was not easy for him to determine, for he had a chronic lung problem that always threatened his life. In fact, he was again very close to death when he spent three-and-a-half months in a tuberculosis sanitarium in 1967. He recovered well and thereafter continued to work for others' welfare with great energy. He took responsibility for an increased number of students and built Labsum Shedrub Ling's retreat house and schoolhouse with his own hands and his students' assistance. In the winters he had cold-induced asthma which frequently brought on pneumonia. It seemed clear to his students that his damaged lungs would eventually cause his death. To stave off that eventuality, some of his students invited him to warmer climates during the winter, starting in 1976. Finally, a group of his students bought a house in southern Florida for him in 1979. In the years prior to his death in January of 1983, he would move there with a few students for the coldest winter months.

In Florida, Geshe-la would constantly remind us that when it was time for him to die, there would be no place from which to escape death. Therefore, when he contracted pneumonia in the summer of 1982, his words seemed to be coming true. But the weather was warm, and, as usual, he reacted well to antibiotics. Thus, he was able to recover without much trouble.

Later on that summer he told me that his dreams had never returned to normal after his recent bout with pneumonia. When Geshe-la's dreams were disturbed, he understood it to be a sign that he had some illness. However, as there were no outward signs of illness, I chose to ignore this sign, hoping that Geshe-la would overcome any sickness, as he had done in the past. However, knowing the strength of Geshe-la's awareness of his own impermanence, I am sure that he did not choose to ignore this sign. On the contrary, he read it as confirmation of an approaching death.

This was clear in what he said before he left for Florida. When Geshe-la's lungs started to become affected by the cold weather, he prepared to go south. Before he left, he visited Geshe Dawa Sangbo, one of his monks who was staying at Labsum Shedrub Ling's New Brunswick, New Jersey monastery. Geshe-la said goodbye and then said that he would not see him again. At the time Geshe Dawa Sangbo thought that Geshe-la had made a mistake in his speech. But in retrospect it is now clear to him that Geshe-la was expecting to die.

Part of an awareness mindful of death and impermanence is the readiness to go at any time. It is said that one who has this awareness is like a person who is going on a trip, and the one who does not have it is like one who is staying behind.[6] The best preparation for death is to practice Buddha's teaching, for one's practice is the only thing that one can take to the next life. Actualizing Buddha's teaching was Geshe-la's one-pointed focus. An aspect of this actualization was his non-attachment to worldly concerns, such that he was packed and ready to go at any time. Geshe-la manifested this aspect very clearly in his final months.

In October of 1982 Geshe-la transferred ownership of the Labsum Shedrub Ling monastery building in New Brunswick, New Jersey to the Tibet Fund, a charitable organization directly under the guidance of His Holiness the Fourteenth Dalai Lama of Tibet. Geshe-la had been preparing for this event for almost two years. He had a special relationship with His Holiness and held him in great reverence as one of his root lamas. In an audience that I had in 1985 with His Holiness in Dharmsala, India, His Holiness himself appeared surprised when describing the closeness of their relationship. He thought that it must have stemmed from the historical relationship of the Dalai Lamas and the Mongolians.[7]

Geshe-la intended the building as an offering to His Holiness, saying that he knew that His Holiness was far more able than he to do something with the building that would be of benefit to others. It was a large building and represented almost half of Labsum Shedrub Ling's assets. At the official ceremony to mark the occasion on October 17th, Geshe-la said in his speech that he considered this offering the culmination of his life's work. After giving his speech, he sat down and rubbed his hands in a gesture of conclusion of work well-done, reciting the Sanskrit phrase, "Sarva mangalam" ["May all beings be happy."] This phrase is often written at the end of Tibetan scriptures, and I had never seen Geshe-la do this on any other occasion.

Thus, before going to Florida, Geshe-la brought his life's work to a conclusion and was prepared for death. Of course, as Geshe-la would say in response to his students' requests for him to stay to accomplish his work, "There is no end to doing things." And as I have said, he did not stop teaching until his last breath. But, in a life dedicated to helping others, his offering to His Holiness was a culmination, for he gave without attachment a large portion of what he had worked his whole life to accumulate, and he gave it within the thought of others' greater benefit. In conclusion, he had dedicated to the happiness of others all the merit that he had accumulated from that act of giving.

Geshe-la's preparation for death even extended to being in control of the circumstances of his death. When he told Geshe Dawa Sangbo that he was going to his death, he was choosing a place to die. The Florida house was a place where he could retreat from his work and find relative peace. Ironically, it was the place that we, his students, had chosen for the sake of extending his life. It was as if Geshe-la was underlining his statement that when it was time for him to die, there would be no place from which to escape his death.

The Florida house was also a place where Geshe-la could be free of the physical discomforts of his asthma. However, once freed of his lung problems, he had symptoms of a new illness. That illness proved to be cancer of the liver and colon. Geshe-la refused to seek treatment in a hospital, a policy that he had made known to his students since his return from the tuberculosis sanitarium, for he knew very well that he would give up any control of his situation if he went to a hospital. Instead, he was attended by physicians who were his own students, Dr. Peter Beskyd and Dr. Philip Hauptman. My wife, Diana, and I attended him as nurses.

From the time I came to stay with him in 1970, Geshe-la had constantly told his students what to do at the time of his death. Diana had come in 1972. Since arriving, we had both served him by attending to his personal needs, as well as assisting him in his work and receiving his teachings. Therefore, he had trained us well concerning what he would need when sick and dying. He could be confident that we would provide what he needed even if it became too difficult for him to talk.

Geshe-la always emphasized the importance of the moment of death. It is a crucial juncture for the Buddhist practitioner, because the attitude at the moment of death determines where one is to be reborn. A virtuous state of mind assures a happy transmigration to the life of a human or god, whereas a non-virtuous one means a bad transmigration to the life of an animal, hungry ghost, or hell being. Geshe-la often cautioned his students against weeping when he was dying, for such actions might cause desire to arise in his mind, endangering his transmigration. Instead, he asked us to recite the mantra of Avalokiteshvara, *oṃ maṇi padme hūṃ*. He also expressed the wish to die looking towards an image of Shakyamuni Buddha. In this way he would be assured of a good state of mind at death.

An incident between Geshe-la and I in the first years that I studied with him is a good metaphor for his careful preparation for the crucial and dangerous moment of death. We were working together, burning a pile of brush in the middle of the driveway. It was a difficult day for burning, and there was the constant danger of the fire getting out of control. I was very impressed by Geshe-la's control. He very carefully put on branches and made sure that any sticks to the outside were brought into the middle. He never put on too many pieces of brush such that the flames rose too high. We waited until it completely burned, and then poured water on the ashes. When the situation needed great care, Geshe-la could apply it very meticulously. That is the way he approached the moment of death.

Until the final month, it was not clear to us that he had a terminal disease. Although he said that he was dying, he had said so when sick many times in the past. Geshe-la spent his time reading and instructing his students much as he did in the past.

But finally he was very direct about his situation and started to put much of his energy into preparing for when he would not be around. He spent about two weeks working on a memorandum that contained final instructions for the administration of Labsum Shedrub Ling. He sat me down in his room and told me point blank that he was dying. He thereafter gave me verbal instructions on what to do in order to continue his work. He read a scripture on mind transference (*'pho ba*)[8] that he had always kept with him. He composed his legal will to pass on a few personal possessions. He even spent time with Diana to pack his clothes into his suitcases.

During the final month of his life, Geshe-la would try to keep active. He took an occasional walk and went for rides in the car. Ten days before his death, he even played chess as well as ever. He kept up his daily morning prayers until the final two days. This was all an incredible feat of strength, considering the great burden of his suffering.

One incident in particular highlighted the fact of Geshe-la's suffering as well as his continued desire to live. One week before he died, Geshe-la asked Dr. Beskyd to visit from New York. Although Dr. Hauptman was in constant attendance and Geshe-la was for the most part his own doctor, he had great respect for Dr. Beskyd's advice. When Dr. Beskyd arrived, Geshe-la asked him if he could do something to ease the intense suffering. Up to this time Geshe-la had never made it clear that his misery was so difficult to bear. Dr. Beskyd prescribed a mild pain killer. Geshe-la took one tablet in the course of the day and it seemed to help. That night he had a dream in which he was telling his students that he was recovering from his illness, much to his great surprise.

The next morning he called Diana and me into his room, related the dream, and asked if it was possible that the medicine would cure such an intense illness. We told him that the medicine was only for relieving pain. He later told Diana how much he wanted to recover and how disappointed he was that the dream was not true. He also refused to take any more of the pain killers.

Geshe-la resisted his great suffering with his strong will to live, but to live for the sake of others. Often sick persons succumb to a self-centered concern for their own welfare. I was always amazed that whenever Geshe-la became sick, he sustained his constant concern for others. If anything, his altruistic attitude was more pronounced.

His terminal illness was no exception. He constantly attended to his students' concern over his condition, and he continued to teach each according to what was helpful to him or her at that time. When some called, he would let them know that he was praying for them. When others would want to visit, he would ask them to pray at home. One, whom he had not seen for a while, he asked to come to visit. In the same way, he would accept or refuse medicines and advice. He wanted to spare his students the sight of his suffering and himself the sight of their unhappiness. He was greatly concerned for those who attended him. For example, two days before his death, Geshe-la began to bleed internally. By this time he barely had the energy to talk, yet he told us to take a swim at the beach, because he was worried that we were becoming too unhappy at the sight of his misery.

It was only during these final two days that Geshe-la was bedridden. Up to this point one of us had always stayed in the room nearby and frequently looked in on him. For three weeks I had been spending the nights on a mattress in his room. Now we made sure that someone was always in the room. At 11:00 P.M. on January 29th he sat up in his bed and told me that he was in the final stages of the dying process. Of course, he did not have the energy to tell me what this meant, but I assumed that we should start to recite gently the mantra, *oṃ maṇi padme hūm*. He was very pleased when we did this.

The next morning I brought in a painting of Buddha that His Holiness the Dalai Lama had given Geshe-la in 1979 on the occasion of his first visit to the United States and Labsum Shedrub Ling. Previous to this, Geshe-la would not allow me to bring any holy objects into his room because his condition prevented him from keeping the room clean enough. Now I made sure that the image was always in his view, no matter what side of the room he was turned towards.

Geshe-la died at 4:25 that afternoon. We were greatly concerned that he would slip into a coma before-hand (a common occurrence with liver cancer), but that was not the case. He was too fortunate and too strong for that to happen; he was clearminded to the last breath. In that last moment he looked at me and smiled, turned his head and looked at the painting of Buddha, and, peacefully closing his eyes, let go of his last breath.

Above all else, Geshe-la was a teacher. He once said to a group of his students, "When I die, you will understand." He was teaching us throughout his illness and death. He taught that the burden of illness can be used to increase our thoughts for others. He showed that death will certainly come, that it entails much suffering, and that we must maintain our will to live while being accepting of our death. He emphasized that it is a crucial time for which one must always be ready. Proper preparation begins with a cultivation of an awareness mindful of impermanence and death, which then serves as a basis for attaining good qualities through actualizing Buddha's teachings. He showed how to die, but, more importantly, how to live. If we follow these teachings, there will be no reason for regret at the moment of death, and we will face it with optimism, just as

Geshe Pu-chung-wa said:

> At that time [of death] the measure of our knowledge, our strength, and the wisdom of our goals will be clear. When we face death happily and with joyful anticipation, we are wise, strong; our goals are noble, and we will enter death clear-headed.

1 Origins of the Teaching

The *Commentary on (Ɖzong-ka-ɓa's) "Foundation of All Excellence"* (*yon tan gzhir gyur ma'i 'grel pa*) says:

> At the beginning of his spiritual career, the great being who was to become known as Shakyamuni Buddha first generated the altruistic aspiration to highest enlightenment in both its aspirational and practical forms. Then for three incalculable great aeons he accumulated the collections of merit and wisdom, which consist of the six perfections. He then attained the perfection of life, Buddhahood, for the sake of all living beings.
>
> He next imparted to his disciples the precious nectar of the holy teaching with all its eighty-four thousand aggregates. By this act he set all beings on the right path, maturing those who were not yet mature, liberating those who were mature, and bringing to perfection those who were liberated.
>
> All Buddha's essential teachings are included in the "lam rim" teachings — teachings on the stages of the path to enlightenment. There are many benefits in hearing and studying this teaching; to name just a few, one will understand the entire teaching, turn away from

41

wrongdoing, give up senseless activities, and attain nirvana.

Shakyamuni Buddha, great spiritual friend of all beings in the universe, became a supreme treasury of precious, inconceivable knowledge and excellence.[9] He illuminated the true path to the high states of humans and gods and to the final goal of perfect enlightenment. By the great lion's roar of his teaching on dependent-arising (*rten byung, pratītyasamutpāda*), this greatly merciful teacher overcame the fox-like teachers of mistaken doctrines.

When in former lives he undertook the practices of a Bodhisattva, he saw the entire universe enveloped in a thick darkness of ignorance. Beings were suffering in the abyss of birth, old age, sickness, and death, overpowered by various afflictive emotions that were like poisonous snakes or wild animals. Having fallen into the swamp of cyclic existence wherein their minds and bodies were tormented in many ways, they cried out pitifully. He, correctly seeing this with his unsurpassed mercy and compassion, provided them with the sustenance of happiness and help by listening to them, deeply considering their conditions, and directly assisting them.

Because this Bodhisattva who was to become Shakyamuni Buddha had actualized the precious altruistic aspiration to enlightenment (*byang chub kyi sems, bodhicitta*), he cherished all beings more than himself and constantly desired only to free them from their sufferings. Having promised to accomplish this desire, he worked for many lives over thousands of aeons without any regard for his life and body. Motivated by such an attitude, his actions were completely contrary to the common ways of the world. Merely hearing of such difficult practice brings fear to ordinary persons not inclined to religion.

With courageous and persistent effort, the Bodhisattva completed the collections of both merit and wisdom, freeing himself from the obstructions (*sgrib pa, āvaraṇa*) that prevent liberation and omniscience, and attaining the high state of Buddhahood. Just as a wishfulfilling jewel is able to fulfill all desires, so he was now able to fulfill his own ultimate aim and to help others fulfill theirs. He was now Shakyamuni Buddha, Dharma-king of the three realms. All his acts and thoughts arose spontaneously, powered by his previous generation of the aspiration to enlightenment and ocean of supplicating prayers. Soon, beginning with his birth in Tushita paradise, he was to display the many forms of a Buddha's twelve deeds throughout this universe containing billions of world systems.[10] He was to liberate his disciples in accordance with their thoughts, dispositions, and latent inclinations and to illuminate completely the darkness of the three realms with the light of his virtuous activities, a great treasure.

After emanating from Tushita paradise, Shakyamuni Buddha took birth on the continent of India, named Jambudvipa. He was born a prince of the royal caste, the caste respected above all others. However, he gave up administration of the kingdom and left his palace, taking a vow of renunciation. He then took on arduous practice of asceticism for six years. Finally, subduing the devils, he reenacted his former attainment of Buddhahood, manifesting perfect enlightenment in a single night while seated beneath the bodhi tree.

As a manifest Buddha, he continued the display of his twelve deeds by turning the three wheels of the dharma, or teaching. Initially the great gods Brahma and Indra requested him to turn the wheel of the teaching. He then taught the first wheel of the teaching, known as "the wheel of the four noble truths", to his first five disciples in the forest of Varanasi called Deer Park. At this time Buddha expounded the four noble truths and taught the true existence of phenomena. Then, at Vulture Peak, he turned the second wheel of the teaching for the benefit of innumerable disciples — Bodhisattvas, Hearers, gods, and humans. This second teaching explained the view of emptiness, or the lack of true existence (*bden par grub pa, satyasiddhi*), and was known as "the middle wheel of signlessness". Finally, to a similar group of disciples, he taught the third wheel of the teaching, known as "the wheel which distinguishes well" (the previous two teachings); at that time he explained the details and significance of differentiating true existence and lack of true existence with regard to the three natures.[11]

In this way the Supramundane Victor (*bcom ldan 'das, bhagavān*) realized and set forth the three wheels of the teaching in order to reverse the discordant conditions known as the afflictive emotions. There are eighty-four thousand aspects of these afflictions, which are divided into four groups of twenty-one thousand each. These groups deal respectively with desire, hatred, ignorance, and all three together. To counteract these activities, Buddha taught the eighty-four thousand aspects of the teaching.

According to their manner of expression the scriptures are divided into twelve components: (1) discourses, (2) songs, (3) prophecies (4) verses, (5) purposeful statements, (6) summaries, (7) hagiography, (8) legends, (9) birth stories, (10) vast texts, (11) miraculous qualities, and (12) delineations.

In terms of subject matter, the scriptures are divided into the three collections (*sde snod gsum, tripiṭaka*). That which chiefly sets forth as its subject matter training in exceptional ethics is called the collection of moral discipline. The next two collections with their trainings in exceptional meditative stabilization and exceptional wisdom are called, respectively, the collection of discourses and the collection of manifest knowledge. Among the twelve components of scripture, the first five are included in the collection of discourses, the next four in the collection of moral discipline, and the remaining three in the collection of Mahayana discourses. Among all twelve sections, statements concerning specifically characterized (*rang mtshan, svalakṣaṇa*) and generally characterized (*spyi mtshan, sāmānyalakṣaṇa*) phenomena belong to the collection of manifest knowledge.

After the Supramundane Victor had turned the three wheels of the teaching, he indicated Mahakashyapa as his successor. After this, in order to lead eternalists towards the teaching, he showed the last of his twelve deeds by entering final nirvana. His teachings were sufficient for his disciples, and his time was at an end. He passed on.

Mahakashyapa then assembled five hundred Arhats, the great teachers of the spiritual community, for the first council of the teaching. This was held during the three month summer retreat, when monks were prohibited from leaving the monastery grounds. At that time the Arhats asked Ananda, Buddha's close disciple and servant, to speak first. Because there was no throne from which to preach, the other four hundred and ninety-nine Arhats piled up their yellow religious robes to make a throne. Ananda sat upon this and, placing his hands together in prayer, faced the direction of Buddha's place of final nirvana and, overwhelmed by strong feelings, burst into tears of deeply felt emotion. In a beautiful voice filled with sadness he began his recitation of the teachings with these words, "Thus have I heard..." In this way, the council brought together the great collection of discourses.

After Ananda had finished, he descended from the throne. Upali took his place and began a recitation of the collection of moral discipline. After him, the leader of the council, Mahakashyapa, came forward and recited the collection of manifest knowledge. These three collections constituted the first collecting of Buddha's word.

Shortly thereafter, Mahakashyapa bequeathed the position of successor to Ananda and passed away. Subsequently the line of succession passed from Ananda to Shanavasika, from him to Upagupta, and then to Dhitika, Kṛṣhna, and Sudarshana. These were the first seven successors to Buddha Shakyamuni.

The second council of the teaching came one hundred and ten years after Buddha's final nirvana. At that time, the monks in Vaishali were taking delight in ten activities prohibited for monks. At this second council, Buddha's followers purified the Buddha's teaching of the defilements caused by these monks, performing an auspicious ceremony of purification. At that time, the gods proclaimed from the sky:

> The non-religious factions are defeated.
> Religion is victorious!

Two different reports of the third council of teaching are recorded in the commentaries. The first is that one hundred and thirty-seven years after Buddha's final nirvana, in the city of Pataliputra, a devil manifested himself as an Arhat. He displayed a variety of miraculous deeds in order to create a schism in the spiritual community. This schism lasted for sixty years. Then a monk named Vatsiputra called the order together, dispelled disagreement, and brought the peace of the teaching to the community.

The second report describes an event that occurred one hundred and sixteen years after Buddha's final nirvana. In the Indian city of Kusumito (*me tog gis rgyas pa*) were four monks who recited the scriptures in four different Sanskrit dialects. Thereby, the disciples of these monks came to be divided into four main sects. Their disagreements eventually led to a division into eighteen sects. At one time they discovered a sutra in which Buddha told of the prophetic dream of King Krikri. Therein Buddha interpreted the dream to mean that although his teaching would be divided into eighteen sects, the teaching of liberation would not degenerate. Seeing this, they put aside their differences and assembled to collect Buddha's teaching. From the viewpoint of the general vehicle (that which is common to all followers), this last council ends the period of compiling Buddha's teaching.

The original compilers of the Mahayana teaching were Bodhisattvas such as Maitreya. As Bhavaviveka states in his *Blaze of Reasoning* (*rtog ge 'bar ba, tarkajvālā*):

> The gatherers, or compilers, of the fundamental

Mahayana teachings are Samantabhadra, Manjushri, Vajrapani, Maitreya, and so on. Hearers could not compile them because they do not study Mahayana scriptures.

The Mahayana teachings of secret mantra (*tantrayāna*) were compiled by Vajrapani and the dakinis.[12] The tantras' description of how this took place differs greatly from that found in the sutras.

After Shakyamuni Buddha had entered final nirvana, many disciples in India practiced the Mahayana system internally without revealing this to others. Because not many followers were externally teaching or receiving the Mahayana scriptures in India at that time, the canons were carried away by the gods and nagas who followed Buddha's teaching. This precious teaching was purified by the great gods and nagas. They respected it greatly, bearing it like an ornament upon the crown of their heads. In this way, they cleared away all defilements from this realm. Again, from Bhavaviveka's *Blaze of Reasoning*:

> Not long ago after Buddha entered final nirvana, the Hearers and other Hinayana practitioners became very attached to the teachings they had received. The compilers brought together only those sections of the teaching that accorded with their own inclinations. No one collected the Mahayana scriptures, for there was no one who was a proper vessel for that practice. The Mahayana teachings were collected by the nagas, and so on, and taken to their country. Thus, they became the vessels for its practice. Later, Nagarjuna, who was prophesied by Buddha, collected the Mahayana teachings from the land of the nagas and spread them throughout the human realm.

It is clear that the second dissemination of the Mahayana teachings occurred after the great teacher Arya Nagarjuna came to India. The Mahayana teaching that was first systematized by Nagarjuna became widely recognized as the correct path to enlightenment. Through it, one can attain Buddha's own form of perception. Yet, before one is motivated to make effort at this, it is necessary analytically to understand the correctness of Buddha's realization. Thus we need now to consider the basis for recognizing Buddha as a valid source of knowledge.

2 Establishing Buddha as a Perfectly Right Being

The *Commentary on (Dzong-ka-ba's) "Foundation of All Excellence"* says:

> The very root of the path to enlightenment is the practice of reliance on a spiritual teacher. Buddha stated in sutra that to rely properly on the spiritual teacher, one must conceive of oneself as a sick person, of the spiritual teacher as the doctor, of his precepts as the medicine, and of earnest practice as the cure. To increase one's faith in the spiritual teacher, Buddha said that one must rely on him with a mind that is like earth, never tired of its burden; with a mind immutable as a diamond, never changing in its resolve; and with a mind like a devoted attendant, doing all tasks without having to be told.

Proper reliance on a spiritual teacher requires conviction that Buddha himself, the original teacher and model for all Buddhist teachers, attained complete, valid realization.[13] Dignaga, in his *Compendium on Right Perception (tshad ma kun btus, pramāṇasamuccaya)* uses two methods of reasoning to establish that the teacher, Buddha, is a perfectly right being (*tshad ma'i skyes bu, pramāṇa puruṣa*). In his salutation to that work, Dignaga presents the basis for establishing Buddha's correctness.

An explanation of Dignaga's salutation that proceeds from the first word to the last is the sequential ordering and that proceeding from the last word to the first is the reverse ordering. Dignaga's salutation is as follows:[14]

> I bow down to the one who became perfectly right,
> The helper of beings, teacher, Sugata, and rescuer.

In these two lines, Dignaga offers a very precise salutation to the Buddha. By saying, "the one who became perfectly right," Dignaga indicates the teacher, Buddha. More specifically, with the words "one who became", Dignaga refutes the non-Buddhist belief in permanent, or unchangeable, self-arisen right perception. In saying "the helper of beings", Dignaga indicates great compassion; "teacher" signifies the wisdom that cognizes selflessness (*bdag med, nairātmya*); "Sugata" (One Gone to Bliss — i.e., a Buddha), indicates a Sugata who is endowed with either the three aspects of abandonment or the three aspects of realization (see below); and "rescuer" indicates how Buddha acts as a refuge.

Using the first epithet of his salutation as the basis and the remaining four as distinguishing characteristics, Dignaga shows how to establish that Buddha is a perfectly right being. Dignaga had a reason for using the epithet "teacher" to indicate the wisdom that cognizes selflessness. For, Buddha saves living beings from suffering through his unmistaken teaching of the method for liberation, and such teaching arises through the force of wisdom, its main cause. In order that this process might be understood, Dignaga designated the cause (the wisdom cognizing emptiness) with the name of the effect (the teacher).

If we take the salutation's distinguishing characteristics sequentially, Dignaga indicates that the Sugata is endowed with complete abandonment (of afflictive emotions). This is done to show that Buddha had to free himself from suffering before liberating others. In the reverse ordering of the salutation's distinguishing characteristics, Dignaga indicates that the Sugata is endowed with complete realization. He does this in order to make clear that Buddha needed to know how to liberate others from suffering before he could actually do so. Thus, in the sequential ordering, Dignaga indicates liberation and in the reverse ordering, omniscience.

A Sugata's abandonment and realization each have three aspects. In terms of abandonment, a Sugata has:

1 good abandonment
2 irreversible abandonment
3 complete abandonment.

These aspects of abandonment elevate the Sugata who has accomplished them above, respectively, 1) a non-Buddhist, 2) a Stream Enterer (*rgyun zhugs, srotāpanna*) who must return to cyclic existence seven times, and 3) a Self-Enlightened Arhat (*rang sangs rgyas dgra bcom pa, pratyeka-buddha arhat*) or a Hearer Arhat (*nyan thos dgra bcom pa, śrāvaka arhat*).[15]

In terms of realization a Sugata has:

1 realization of reality
2 firm realization
3 complete realization.

These three aspects elevate the realized Sugata above, respectively, 1) a non-Buddhist, 2) a learner,[16] and 3) a Self-Enlightened or Hearer Arhat.

To repeat Dignaga's salutation:

> I bow down to the one who became perfectly right,
> The helper of beings, teacher, Sugata, and rescuer.

What are the sequential and reverse orderings of this salutation? The former is the method of teaching that, following the order of the salutation, indicates that from compassion arises the wisdom that cognizes selflessness, from this wisdom arises the Sugata having the three aspects of abandonment, and from the Sugata arises the rescuer. Called the sequential ordering because it follows the sequence of generation, it thereby establishes that subsequent effects arise from their respective antecedent causes. It is an explanation of an effect through observation of its causes.

The other side of this is the reverse ordering, beginning from the last word of the salutation, which explains the causes of Buddhahood through observation of the effects. Here one establishes that Shakyamuni Buddha attained a Sugata's three aspects of realization because he is a rescuer. One can establish that Buddha generated the wisdom cognizing selflessness because he attained the realization of a Sugata. Because Buddha has that wisdom, one can establish Buddha's preceding attainment of great compassion. This method of teaching through establishment of antecedent causes is called teaching the order of realization because it shows the order of inferred antecedent causes through analysis of their subsequent effects.

With respect to the "order of realization", all correct reasons are, in general, means of inferring that which is being established (*sgrub bya, sādhya*). More specifically, the latter three reasons given above are "effect reasons" (*'bras rtags, phalahetu*) whereby the existence of a cause is definitively inferred through the existence of its effect, just as the presence of fire is inferred through the existence of its effect, smoke.

Here, establishing the teacher as perfectly right and as omniscient (*rnam pa thams cad mkhyen pa, sarvākārajñāta*) are said to be similar. Just as a right perception (*tshad ma, pramāṇa*) is right with regard to its object, so Buddha is right with regard to teaching beings how to liberate themselves from suffering. Thus, Buddha is established as a perfectly right being.

Furthermore, the omniscience that is established here is not Buddha's knowing purposeless facts such as the number of living beings in the ocean, but his unmistaken know-.

ledge of and skill in the method of liberating beings from suffering. It is this omniscience that is most significant for the practice of those intent on liberation.

Both the sequential and reverse (inductive and deductive) orderings yield explanations establishing that Buddha is an omniscient (or perfectly right) being. The former enables one to understand what path the teacher travelled; this refutes opponents who say there is no cause that could create, or lead to, omniscience (that is, that omniscience does not exist). The latter shows how Buddha progressed on the path he travelled; this refutes opponents who say that there is no cause for the attainment of omniscience (that is, that omniscience is uncaused). Both these approaches are established by reasoning.

SEQUENTIAL ORDERING ESTABLISHING THE TEACHER AS A PERFECTLY RIGHT BEING

A. The Purpose for the Reasoning of the Sequential Ordering
Nihilists maintain there is no cause that can create an omniscient being. They reason as follows: Neither an omniscient nor perfectly right being exists because, in order to be omniscient, one must know all hidden phenomena (*lkog gyur, parokṣa*), and such knowledge cannot be proved. This follows because such omniscience arises after meditating for many lifetimes; one cannot attain it in a single life. This is impossible, nihilists reason, because there are no former or future lifetimes. Furthermore, if one made great effort at cultivating compassion for a long time, one could increase compassion somewhat but could never increase it limitlessly because all training has a certain limit. This is exemplified by high-jumping or heating water. No matter how much you heat water, its temperature cannot increase beyond a certain point.

To the assertions of nihilists, Dharmakirti, the "Lord of Reasoning", replies as follows: Both of your examples are incorrect. Suppose that you have trained at high-jumping once with great effort. When you jump again, you must again make an effort just as you did previously — the latter jump cannot arise spontaneously from the former. By contrast, when you familiarize yourself with compassion and so on, you need *not* make a new effort similar to the first effort in order to produce a continuation of that compassionate mental state. You are able to produce many similar continuations on the basis of your previous effort. Thus you can increase compassion limitlessly.

When we heat water too much, its basis — the water — evaporates. This is due to the instability of water. The mind on which compassion and so on are based is stable, however, in that the continuation of just the mind's clear knowing never ceases.

Therefore, in order to increase familiarization limitlessly, both a stable basis and independence from renewed efforts are required. Because high-jumping lacks the latter and heating water lacks the former, they cannot increase limitlessly. Because the cultivation of compassion has both these conditions in complete form, it will increase in accordance with how much we cultivate it.

Hence, it is correct to say that familiarization which depends on the mind increases limitlessly. If defilements such as the conception of self (*bdag tu 'dzin pa, ātmagraha*) were ingrained in the nature of the mind, they could not be destroyed unless the mind itself were destroyed, just as heat cannot be separated from fire. But such defilements are not ingrained in the nature of the mind; they arise adventitiously. We can be freed from defilements because they are superimposed temporarily on the mind due to our ignorance. This process is like cooling a piece of red-hot iron by separating it from fire.

Because this is so, we can use reasoning to refute the referent object (*zhen yul*) of the *conception of self*. Based on that refutation, we are able to generate an ascertaining consciousness (*nges shes, niścayajñāna*) which realizes the non-existence of that referent object. Once we accustom ourselves repeatedly to extending that ascertaining consciousness, we are able to achieve through reasoning the clear appearance of selflessness.

The reason for this is as follows: The wisdom that realizes the selflessness of persons by means of a mental image (*don spyi, arthasāmānya*) is ready to observe an actual, clear appearance of the object of meditation when one has meditated in conjunction with the conditions for meditation for a long time. This is so because that wisdom has a stable basis and is a wholesome mental quality which does not require renewed effort once it has been cultivated. An example of something renewable without increased effort is desire.[17] Its "basis" is just the mind's clear knowing. The reasoning which proves that no beginning or end can be found to just knowing establishes that such knowing is stable.[18]

B. How the Sequential Ordering Explicitly Establishes the Teacher as Omniscient

There are four proof statements in this section:

1. The Bodhisattva who is to become Shakyamuni Buddha in a future life and who has just attained the accumulation path (*tshogs lam, sambhāramārga*) is suitable to generate the wisdom directly cognizing selflessness (a quality indicated in Dignaga's salutation by the word "teacher"). This is established because he is a beginning Bodhisattva who has come under the influence of great compassion (a quality indicated in Dignaga's salutation by the word "helper"). The Bodhisattva is like a skillful doctor who, influenced by compassion, wishes to cure the illness of his patients and is intent on the method for doing so.[19]

2. The Bodhisattva who is to become Shakyamuni Buddha in a future life and who is on the path of seeing's (*mthong lam, darśanamārga*) release path (*rnam grol lam, vimuktimārga*) is able to generate a Sugata having the three aspects of abandonment (a quality indicated by the word "Sugata" in Dignaga's salutation). This is so because he is a Bodhisattva on the path of seeing directly cognizing selflessness. He is like a skillful doctor who cures his patient's illness.[20]

3. The Buddha Superior (*'phags pa, ārya*) who is to be known as Shakyamuni Buddha and who abides in the first instant of omniscience is able to help others attain their ultimate purpose (a quality indicated in Dignaga's salutation by the word "rescuer"). This is because he has attained the final abandonment having three aspects. He is like a skillful doctor who saves a patient's life without regard for gain, respect, or other worldly concerns.[21]

4. Our teacher is a perfectly right being to lead those intent on liberation; that is, he is an omniscient being who knows completely the methods of liberation from suffering. This is so because he has perfected the ability to save others by unmistakenly teaching them, through his compassion, the method of liberation from suffering just as he has realized it himself. One who has omniscient knowledge about methods of liberation is like a skillful doctor who, without confusing the stages of application, administers the medicine that destroys sickness and establishes the patient in the happiness of health.[22]

HOW THE REVERSE ORDERING ESTABLISHES BUDDHA AS OMNISCIENT

Eternalists say there is no cause for the attainment of omniscience. They say an omniscient being exists but does not know all individual phenomena. Rather, he is called "omniscient" because he creates all things. For example, a person who knows how to make many things with his hands is, in general usage, called "all-knowing" or, you can say, "omniscient" in his craft. Thus the creator of all worlds, the Lord God who is self-arisen and eternal, knows all. However, no cause exists which can give rise to omniscience because there is no method for causing one who previously did not know everything to know it later. For instance, those who are unaware that a demon is right in front of them cannot locate it no matter how they may try.

In order to refute these misconceptions of eternalists, Dharmakirti uses the reverse ordering to prove that Buddha is an omniscient being. Again there are four proof statements:

1. The Supramundane Victor frees from suffering those intent on liberation because he knows well the unmistaken method for doing so and teaches accordingly and without error.[23]

2. The Supramundane Victor must have attained previously his own cause — the state of a Sugata having the three aspects of realization. This is true because he has become a rescuer, able to help others attain their ultimate purpose and to teach them without error the discarding included in the first two noble truths and the adopting included in the last two noble truths.[24]

3. The Buddha Superior, known as the Supramundane Victor, who abides in the first instant of omniscience, must have previously attained his cause — the wisdom that directly cognizes selflessness — because he has attained the state of a Sugata having the three aspects of realization.[25]

4. The Bodhisattva on the path of seeing who will become the Supramundane Victor in a future life must have previously generated the great compassion that is the cause of his high state because he is a Bodhisattva Superior who directly cognizes selflessness.[26]

Not all of the syllogisms, or proof statements, just described are exactly syllogisms for establishing Buddha as a perfectly right being, for they do not all explicitly mention perfectly right being as the object whose existence they are proving. However, all the syllogisms either directly or indirectly prove that Buddha is a perfectly right being.

THE PURPOSE OF PROVING THE TEACHER IS OMNISCIENT OR PERFECTLY RIGHT

Intelligent persons might think, "Buddha indicated such teachings as the discarding and adopting set forth by the four noble truths as the method for liberating beings from suffering. Did Buddha teach those methods after first understanding them himself or not?"

To investigate this one could make the following proof statement. Just after attaining Buddhahood, Buddha explained discarding and adopting in the context of the four noble truths and so forth. His explanation of these methods of liberation must have been preceded by a complete knowledge of them, because it is a correct expression that unmistakenly indicates those methods. For example, Buddha's teaching of the selflessness of persons is an unmistaken method for attaining liberation.[27]

The purpose of proving Buddha's omniscience is to show that he is a suitable refuge. In general, the two principal reasons for not being a suitable refuge are: (1) not knowing the method of saving oneself from fear, and (2) though knowing that method, not teaching it to others. The following proof statement refutes the idea that a Buddha has such undesirable qualities: The omniscient Buddha, as established by the sequential ordering, knows well those methods for liberation from suffering because he has realized them himself and, in accordance with that realization, teaches them to others through his compassion. This shows that Buddha both has the ability to be a refuge and acts as a refuge.

How is that? Buddha realizes the path of liberation unmistakenly because he has attained complete abandonment, exhaustively dispelling the obstructions that hinder the path. Thus he can teach the path of liberation unmistakenly because he has realized it unmistakenly.

Some might wonder whether Buddha, though able to teach thus, teaches mistakenly just as a wicked doctor instructs wrongly because of selfish fears that he will not fulfill his own desires for fame and gain. However, Buddha never speaks falsely through attachment to himself because he has attained the fulfillment of his own purpose — the abandonment of attachment, and so on. Might Buddha teach mistakenly through a lack of compassion for others? Buddha does not speak falsely through a lack of compassion because he has accustomed himself to mercy and great compassion by cultivating it for many lifetimes for the sake of others.

Thus, the Supramundane Victor speaks only that which is unmistaken and beneficial and not that which is mistaken and unhelpful. He speaks only that which is helpful, because he has completed the cultivation of compassion. He speaks only that which is unmistaken, because he has completed all knowledge. Hence, Buddha acts as a refuge by his ability to liberate beings from fear and by teaching well the method of liberating oneself from fear. Therefore, only our teacher is a perfectly right being who is a suitable refuge.

EMINENCE OF THE COMMENTARIES ON RIGHT PERCEPTION

To indicate Buddha's achievement, Dignaga stated in his *Compendium on Right Perception*:

> I bow down to the one who became perfectly right,
> The helper of beings, teacher, Sugata, and rescuer.

As an extensive commentary on these words, Dharmakirti composed the second chapter of his *Precise Commentary*, the "Proof of Right Perception". As there is such detailed commentary, complete in just one chapter, it is not necessary to mention other commentators.

In that chapter of the *Precise Commentary*, Dharmakirti teaches the complete stages of the path in sequential order. Our teacher's path began when he first generated the altruistic aspiration for highest enlightenment and culminated when he attained Buddhahood. Thus, the chapter teaches the stages of the Mahayana path. In that same chapter Dharmakirti, using the reverse ordering, indicates extensively how to attain liberation in dependence on the discarding and adopting taught in the four noble truths. Thus the chapter teaches also the stages of the path common to Hinayana and Mahayana.

Furthermore, the Three Jewels of the Mahayana are established in the sequential ordering discussed in this chapter. The Mahayana Buddha Jewel comprises omniscience as well as the Nature Body possessed of the three aspects of abandonment. The Mahayana Spiritual Community Jewel is composed of Bodhisattvas who, motivated by compassion and high resolve, meditate on the wisdom that directly cognizes selflessness. The Mahayana Teaching Jewel is the wisdom that directly cognizes selflessness conjoined with such virtues as the generation of the altruistic aspiration to highest enlightenment.

In addition, Dharmakirti's second chapter indicates, through the reverse ordering, the Three Jewels connected with the Hinayana. Buddha, by way of his teaching discarding and adopting in the four noble truths, is the Buddha Jewel for those of the Hinayana lineage. The Hinayana Spiritual Community Jewel are those holy beings who actualize, through the force of meditating on the selflessness of persons, the cessation that is an abandonment of afflictive emotions. The Hinayana Teaching Jewel is that cessation together with the wisdom that is directed to the selflessness of persons.

To summarize, our teacher reached his high state in the following way. First he thoroughly understood how to establish the existence of the Three Jewels by factual reasoning and then took refuge in the Three Jewels with conviction born from right perception. Thereafter he proved well both the need and ability to achieve perfect enlightenment for the sake of others. Then, generating the altruistic aspiration for enlightenment, he promised to attain perfect enlightenment. Seeing that complete enlightenment arises from the meditative mind that realizes the four noble truths' mode of subsistence, Buddha made effort for many aeons to accumulate the two collections, of merit and wisdom. Finally, he became the ally and refuge of all beings through attaining the state of a Sugata having the three aspects of abandonment.

Because one can determine all the stages of the Hinayana and Mahayana paths by means of Dharmakirti's "Seven

Treatises on Right Perception" along with Dignaga's *Compendium on Right Perception*, it is crucial to realize these treatises as the most eminent commentaries on Buddhist topics.

As Dzong-ka-ba states in his *Great Exposition of the Stages of Mantra (sngags rim chen mo)*:

> Understand that the commentaries of reasoning such as the "Seven Treatises on Right Perception" are the supreme method for generating great respect that is not just words to our teacher, to the teaching — consisting of both verbal exposition and experiential realization — and to practice that accords with those.

Thus, the purpose of Dignaga and Dharmakirti's analysis is not complete unless it motivates one to cultivate Buddha's realization oneself, putting his teachings into practice. As Buddha himself enjoined, this requires careful and reasoned analysis of his teachings, depending on the four reliances and distinguishing which teachings require interpretation and which are definitive.

3 Putting the Teachings Into Practice

The *Commentary on (Dzong-ka-ba's) "Foundation of All Excellence"* says:

> *Having realized that the spiritual teacher is the root of all excellence, by continuous effort of body, speech, and mind, develop great faith that recognizes his knowledge and does not observe in him even the slightest fault. Remember his vast kindness with deep gratitude, and honor him; make offerings to him, respect him in body and speech, and strive to put his teachings into practice.*

In entering practice of Buddha's teaching, it is essential to adopt the four reliances.[28] This means that one learns to:

1. Rely on the teaching (*chos, dharma*) and not on the person who teaches (*gang zag, pudgala*)
2. Rely on the meaning (*don, artha*) and not on the words (*tshig 'bru, vyañjana*)
3. Rely on definitive (*nges don, nīthārtha*) scriptures and not on those requiring interpretation (*drang don, neyārtha*)
4. Rely on exalted wisdom (*ye shes, jñana*) and not on ordinary consciousness (*rnam shes, vijñana*).

Although the four reliances are stated separately, they are

closely related in meaning. Furthermore, these four reliances clearly indicate all of the stages in the practice leading to enlightenment. For, they demonstrate:

1 how to hear
2 how to think
3 how to meditate
4 that it is not enough to just consider hearing, thinking, and meditating separately but rather they must be unified
5 how actually to put that unification into practice.

The following discussion of the four reliances, which accords with explanations given by the great teachers Maitreya and Asanga, emphasizes their close interconnection.

HOW TO HEAR

One should not rely on hypocrites who seem on the surface to be great holy persons and are renowned among the foolish. Rather, one should depend on those whose actions accord with the teaching and who are able to give instructions in the system of the teaching.

Further, when hearing the teaching, one should not pursue merely words without investigation. Rather, one should listen to the actual meaning with special emphasis on the key instructions concerning how to abandon cyclic existence and engage in practices leading to nirvana.

Further, the teachings we receive should not be listened to in the manner of the orthodox members of the two Hearer sects.[29] These persons do not distinguish correctly which teachings are interpretable and which definitive and thus do not understand the subject matter; finally they abandon the definitive Mahayana sutras. What we must do instead when we do not understand is to listen attentively to those experts who know the meaning thoroughly.

The purpose of hearing such teachings is not merely to increase one's own understanding so that, from attachment, one can proclaim oneself as well-versed or because of attraction to debates. Rather, one should depend on the stages of hearing mentioned above and listen with a pure motivation to the method for attaining liberation.

HOW TO THINK

When generating realization through thinking, it is necessary to learn from the words of a teacher who is a perfectly right being, not just from anyone whom we may like. Moreover, the way of learning is not merely to grasp at the teacher's words, but rather to comprehend their meaning through emphasizing logically reasoned analysis. Further, not just any comprehension is sufficient. One must realize, in accordance with the commentaries of such teachers as Nagarjuna, the profound meaning of the definitive scriptures. That is, one must understand the way of emptiness, for this enables one to travel to the city of liberation. Finally, the mind that realizes emptiness cannot hold the view that emptiness is an affirming negation (*ma yin dgag, paryudāsapratiṣedha*); one must realize the emptiness that is a non-affirming negation (*med dgag, prasajyapratiṣedha*), an emptiness which is just the elimination of that which is to be negated, true existence.[30]

To indicate how the first reliance relates to the instructions on thinking, Asanga says in his *Stages of the Bodhisattva* (*byang sa, bodhisattvabhūmi*), "with reasoning." Dzong-ka-ba explains in his *Essence of the Good Explanations* (*legs bshad snying po*):

> If someone asserts a tenet that is contradictory to reasoning, such a proponent must then accept the logical consequence that Buddha is not a perfectly right being.

Furthermore, Shamkarapati states in his *Praise Exceeding That of the Gods* (*lha las phul du byung bar bstod pa, devātiśayastotra*):

> I do not favor Buddha
> I am not angry with Kapila and others,

I uphold as teacher only
He whose words are logical.

Sthiramati clarifies, "The perfectly right being is the bless-
ed Buddha."

To indicate how the second reliance relates to instructions on thinking about the teaching, Asanga says in his
Actuality of the Stages (sa'i dngos gzhi, bhūmivastu):

> Do not be intent just on what we hear, but think
> over the meaning. Comprehend it. Closely examine
> it.

Regarding how the third reliance relates to thinking,
Dzong-ka-ba says in his *Essence of the Good Explanations:*

> The great systematizers — who were prophesied in
> scriptures to be identifiers of the interpretable and
> definitive — explained the meaning of the interpret-
> able and definitive scriptures. They correctly
> brought meaning into realization by means of logic-
> al reasonings that refuted interpreting the meaning
> of definitive scriptures as something else and estab-
> lished their meaning as definite, unsuitable to be
> interpreted otherwise. One should follow their
> realizations in seeking to understand the meaning
> that Buddha actually intended.

The actual import of Buddha's teachings is emptiness, for
to achieve liberation from cyclic existence it is necessary to
realize the emptiness that is included in the three doors of
liberation — emptiness, signlessness, and wishlessness.
Emptiness here is a lack of self-nature (*rang bzhin, svabhāva*). Because this emptiness was never actually produced, it
is signless, or peaceful, from the beginning. Because it will
not actually be produced in the future, it is also wishless, or
birthless. In order to realize these, one must put the
teachings into practice. To practice, one must ascertain the
two kinds of teachings — the definitive and the interpretable.

It is not enough to practice only interpretable teachings. All the great scholars teach that one must hear, think, and meditate on definitive teachings. It is these that are wholly dependable. In his sutras, Buddha gave a variety of teachings to accord with the different capacities of his disciples. Some sutras teach true existence, while others state that things do not truly exist. Some say that things are external, and others say they are not. Therefore, all the sutras cannot be taken literally and thus all are not definitive.

The mere fact that Buddha calls a sutra definitive does not mean it is actually so; we cannot accept literally statements in sutra such as, "This is definitive," or "That is interpretable." Dzong-ka-ba says in his *Essence of the Good Explanations:*

> Rely on distinguishing the definitive and the interpretable. Furthermore, these cannot be distinguished merely on the basis of scriptures that state, "This is definitive," or "This is interpretable."

For instance, the *Sutra Unravelling the Thought* (*mdo sde dgongs 'grel, saṃdhirnirmocana*) says that the second wheel of the teaching requires interpretation whereas, according to the Consequence School (*thal 'gyur pa, prāsaṅgika*),[31] it is actually definitive; the *Sutra Unravelling the Thought* says that the third wheel of the teaching is definitive, whereas it in fact requires interpretation. Thus, we cannot use mere scriptural quotation as a reliable means for identifying the interpretable and definitive. Nor can we distinguish these just by the strength of our intelligence, nor in dependence on the words of many great Indian and Tibetan scholars. Rather, it is said that we must do so by following the teachings of the two great systematizers who were prophesied by Buddha — namely, Nagarjuna and Asanga.

To follow their teachings does not mean just to read their treatises. We must ourselves realize the meanings they set forth by depending on and analyzing how they refute their opponents and establish their undefiled proofs. The ultimate object to be realized is emptiness, the actual import of the teaching. The ultimate method for realizing that is pure analysis of the two systematizers' logical statements of proof.

The fourth reliance as it relates to thinking means not to depend on ordinary conceptions of objects such as forms but rather to rely on the wisdom that rightly understands their final nature.

HOW TO MEDITATE

Many persons make the gravest of errors by holding the great scriptures to be mere explanations of external existence and then neglecting them, just meditating and not studying. They follow only what others proclaim to be precepts for spiritual attainment. However, there is no one more skillful than Buddha. Because he is endowed with wisdom as well as great compassion, whatever he says is for others' benefit and should be put into practice. Therefore, one must understand with faith that his scriptures are the foremost of precepts for spiritual attainment.

There are apparent contradictions in the literal statements of Buddha's teaching. However, once the intention of those statements is investigated, there are actually no contradictions. Hence, we must realize all the teachings as non-contradictory, and in this way, we will gradually be led by the interpretable scriptures and then apply ourselves to the definitive ones. Realizing that the definitive meaning is the quintessence of practice and that the other teachings are aspects of it, we must accept *all* teachings as precepts for spiritual attainment.

Once we have understood all the teachings as precepts, we must practice constantly; nirvana is reached by means of exalted wisdom which completely realizes its objects.

UNIFICATION OF HEARING, THINKING, AND MEDITATING

One who does not rely on the person but extensively hears and relies on the teaching realizes the entire teaching. By relying on the meaning and not on the words, one retains the meaning of what one hears without forgetting it. By relying on the definitive meaning and not the interpretable, one closely investigates Buddha's intention and eradicates mistaken superimpositions (*sgro 'dogs, samāropa*). Thereafter, one gains the realization that arises from thinking over the meaning of what has been heard.

Because one does not rely on an ordinary consciousness, one is not content with merely hearing and thinking. Practicing the meaning of what has been heard, one generates the exalted wisdom that arises from meditation. Thus it is indicated that one must view realization of exalted wisdom as essential and far superior to the mere understanding of the teaching's verbal explanation through hearing and thinking.

PUTTING THE UNIFICATION INTO PRACTICE

One should not focus on whether the teacher is proclaimed to be superior or inferior but on whether the teaching is meaningful. One should listen properly no matter who is teaching. It is not enough to understand the teacher's verbal teaching; rather, one must apply its meaning in all activities of body, speech, and mind. And, it is absolutely necessary to perceive the meaning rightly. In brief, whatever one does in accordance with the instructions given above will serve as a cause for liberation.

Sagya Pandita says in his *Precious Treasury of Good Explanation* (*legs par bshad pa rin po che'i gter*):

> The skillful accept good teaching
> Even from a child,
> Just as one extracts a deer's musk
> Because the smell is fragrant.

Furthermore, Buddha taught the certification by the three analyses in the following verse:

> Monks and scholars should
> Analyze my words well as one would analyze gold
> Through melting, refining, and polishing,
> And adopt them only then —
> Not for the sake of showing me respect.

Kamalashila explains:

> In that verse, "melting" indicates that the teaching must be seen to accord with [i.e., not be contradicted by] direct cognition. "Refining" indicates that the teaching must be seen to accord with inference. "Polishing" indicates that the teaching must be seen to accord with inference through belief.

There are many other renowned subsidiary topics regarding the presentation of the four reliances. No one should think that the simple words above fully explain the four reliances or that this contains complete quintessential instructions for learning Buddha's teaching in the context of these four reliances. I have explained them here only in brief.

To practice in this way requires deep understanding of the necessity for applying the teachings immediately, without procrastination. Gaining this motivation, in turn, requires a precise recognition of our condition as human beings.

4 The Precious Human Life

The *Commentary on (Dzong-ka-ba's) "Foundation of All Excellence"* says:

> For those fortunate persons who rely properly on a spiritual teacher, it is very important to enter the mental practice of contemplating how difficult this human life of leisure and opportunity is to find. This is the first practice for beginning practitioners of Buddha's teaching and produces the motivation to accomplish the holy teaching.
>
> For a beginningless stream of lifetimes we have wandered in leisureless conditions, such as in the three states of unfortunate beings, because of the influence of our actions and afflictive emotions. Now, this one time, we have obtained a human life endowed with both leisure and opportunity. This good fortune is the convergence of a great deal of virtuous karma, such as meeting with a holy spiritual teacher. Because this life is free from the eight conditions of being without leisure, we have the time to practice the teaching. Once we have the ten conditions for opportunity, we have all the inner and outer causes for realizing the teaching.
>
> When we consider the precepts concerning this human

life — the obstacles to obtaining it, its actual nature, its causes and effects, and the examples concerning it — we see how very rare it is. This life is more precious than a universe filled with wish-fulfilling jewels, for it enables us to accomplish the ten virtuous deeds that cause future birth as humans or gods and, beyond that, can even cause attainment of the adamantine body. With this life we can also generate the altruistic aspiration for enlightenment, achieve the six perfections, and fulfill the three trainings [ethics, meditation, and wisdom], which lead to omniscience and the assured good of liberation.

Understanding the importance of this, do not ruin yourself senselessly with inner and outer distractions, such as sleep and laziness, or by heedless involvement in the eight worldly concerns.[32] Always be conscientious. Hearing, thinking, and meditating on Buddha's doctrine by day and by night, generate a mind that desires to take up the essence of the holy teaching in both its aspects of verbal exposition and experiential insight. Once you have applied such thought to practice, strive to use the methods learned to make meaningful this human life with its leisure and opportunity.

The precious opportunity of attaining a human life was discussed by Dzong-ka-ba in the *Concise Meaning of the Stages of the Path*:

> This life which has leisure
> Is more precious than a wishing-jewel.
> So difficult to find, it is as quickly gone as lightning
>   in the sky.
> Thus, realize that all worldly activities
> Are like chaff in the wind,
> And seize the essence of leisure and opportunity day
>   and night.[33]

How valuable is this good human life[34]

Replete with leisure and opportunity?
It is beyond comparison
With anything else of value.

Fill the whole universe with precious jewels
And it would as nothing compared to this priceless human
    life.
Its significance is this:
Whatever we desire —
Temporary aims
Or the purpose of the final goal, Buddhahood —
Can be achieved through this life
And through this life alone.

Is it your wish to attain
The high states of humans and gods?
This can be gained.

Far beyond earthly experience
Are paradises such as
Tushita or Sukhavati.
You may voyage there
In dependence on this life
Of leisure and opportunity.

Through this life, furthermore,
You may attain the joy of liberation:
Complete elimination of suffering —
Birth, illness, old age, and death.

Even Buddhahood,
The highest stage,
Wherein all faults are nullified
And all virtues perfected,
Is attainable in dependence on this life.

Moreover, in accordance with the Tantra Vehicle,
One can unify method and wisdom
Attaining Buddhahood in one short human life.

Dzong-ka-ba, therefore, has said

As did the Indian pandits
Who preceded him
That this life is more precious
Than a wish-fulfilling jewel.

Even when people have the benefit of a precious human life
There are many who do not strive
Either for liberation or the high states of humans or gods.
Instead, their only desires are for
Happiness and pleasure in this life.

It is as if they held in hand a mass of wishing-jewels
But knew not how to use them.
Therefore, seize the purpose of leisure and opportunity
And cast afar the concerns of this life.

The *Great Exposition of the Stages of the Path* (*lam rim chen mo*) and other scriptures illustrate the rarity of a life endowed with leisure and opportunity:

> The precious human life
> Is as unique as the sight of a limbless man astride a
>   wild ass.
> It is seldom found indeed!

Shantideva's *Engaging in the Bodhisattva Deeds* (*spyod 'jug, bodhisattvacāryāvatāra*) says:

> This leisure and opportunity are so rare that
> If we do not now take advantage
> Of their potential for achieving all purposes,
> How can we regain it in the future?

At this time we have achieved a fortunate life.
Virtues practiced now will cause a future precious human
   life.
Yet, it is taught that a good rebirth is rare
Due to the difficulty of guiding body, speech, and mind to
   virtue.
Even more unique
Is the attainment of leisure and opportunity.

Although we already may have accumulated merit
Leading to attainment of leisure and opportunity,
The obstacles to such attainment are many
For our minds are infused with the three mental poisons.[35]
Though these obstacles may not wholly destroy
The sources of leisure and opportunity,
The afflictive emotions are so strong
And our virtue so much weaker
That attainment of a good rebirth is uncertain.

Opportunity means to meet with Buddha's teaching.
This teaching exists in the world at present,
But its appearance is as rare as seeing stars in the bright of
    day.
Contemplating this example, understand
That attainment of a precious human life is rare indeed.

Buddha, who spoke only truth,
Told that beings in the lower, unfortunate rebirths
Are as numerous as particles of dust on earth.
In comparison, beings in fortunate rebirths
Are as few as particles of dust on one's fingernail.

When we consider the lower rebirths,
The number of animals, hungry ghosts, and hell beings are
    limitless.
In comparison, the number of fortunate rebirths —
Humans, demi-gods, and gods — is infinitesimal.

Few as humans are among all living beings,
Fewer still are those entering the door of the teaching.
Again, few as be those who claim to practice religion,
They are innumerable compared with the tiny number
Possessing perfect leisure and opportunity.

Considering these relative numbers
Buddha gave many examples of the rarity of a precious
    human life:
If a great tortoise lived on the ocean floor
And came up only once in a hundred years,

How much chance would it have of passing through
The opening of a yoke that floated on the surface?

If you toss hard lentils
Against a new smooth wall,
How much chance that one will stick?

If you drop mustard seeds
One by one on a upturned needle
How much chance that one will balance on the point?

Through these examples we can understand
The rarity of a human life with perfect leisure and
   opportunity.
We can rely on only this one chance.

Knowing this, can you exist happily
Without extracting this life's essence?
To not do so is like travelling to an isle of abundant
   treasures
And returning empty-handed.

If we waste our lives
On the attractions of this world
It is as if we were
Intentionally returning to an unfortunate rebirth.
As Shantideva and other great teachers have warned,
There is no mistake greater than this.

Not only is a human life
Of leisure and opportunity difficult to attain,
Encountering the doctrine of Dzong-ka-ba is also not easy
And to meet a fully qualified lama
Is rare indeed.

Receiving the teaching is difficult,
But harder still is to understand its undefiled meaning,
Complete in its presentation.

Rare is one having the wisdom to distinguish good from
   evil,

Who uses intelligence to practice the teaching.
Rare are those spiritual friends seeking liberation
Or even those applying resources to the practice of religion.

If, upon hearing of such rarity
One does not abandon worldly activities
And strive to achieve fortunate rebirth and the final goal,
There is no loss greater than this!

Without being overcome by present attractions
May we have the opportunity to complete the profound
    path
For the sake of helping all living beings, our former
    mothers,
Who have always sustained us with kindness.

All sentient beings in the three realms,
The highest and the lowest,
Want not even the slightest misery
And desire only happiness.
This is clear to us all.

Yet, if we fear misery,
We must avoid all wrongdoing
And if we desire happiness
We must cultivate virtues.
Hence the need to distinguish
Which actions to reject and which to adopt.

One skilled in this
Does not confuse
Worldly and religious paths.
Such is known through reasoning
And through the words of Buddha and his followers.

To proceed through the stages of the path
In harmony with the unmistaken teaching
We must contemplate in full
What it means to have leisure and opportunity.
This is why Dzong-ka-ba taught that a life having leisure

Is most important for temporary or final goals
And more precious than a wish-fulfilling jewel.

Time to study and practice the holy teaching,
This is leisure.
There are eight conditions
For being without leisure:
Being born as a hell-being, hungry ghost, animal,
Barbarian or long-lived god,
Possessing wrong views,
Living in an age when no Buddha has visited,
Or being mentally dull.

For example, hell-beings,
Consumed by torments of heat and cold,
Have no leisure to hear the holy teaching.

Savage barbarians
Are worst among those without leisure.
Equating killing with virtue,
Murder and harm of others
Is their actual religion.
Following their evil practices,
A man may marry his mother.
They are highly skilled in their observances
And ingenious in leading others to their ways.
They spread their customs everywhere
And boast of being best of all.

Among wrong views, that of nihilism
Is widely prevalent in this world.
In these days of the degenerate age
The eight conditions for being without leisure
Have spread wide and far.

To have all conditions for practicing the teaching,
This is opportunity.
The attributes of opportunity
Are contemplated
Through a two-fold division,

Each containing five aspects.

First are the opportunities relating to oneself:
To obtain a human body,
To be born in a central country,
To be born with all sense faculties,
To be free from irreversible actions,
And to have faith in the three objects of refuge.

Next are opportunities related to external conditions:
First, the opportunity of a special kind of teacher
Such as Shakyamuni Buddha who has visited this world.
Second, the opportunity of the holy teaching
Which would not exist had Buddha not taught
The three wheels of the teaching while here.
Third, because this is the aeon of one thousand Buddhas,
We have the opportunity of the teaching still remaining.
Fourth is the presence of Buddha's followers
Arising from their confidence that the teaching is true.

The last opportunity required
Is meeting with a holy spiritual teacher
Who has compassion and mercy for others.

Thus, we absolutely must possess
A life with perfect leisure and opportunity;
Please strive to attain it.

With regard to opportunities relating to oneself:
Since we have now met with the holy teaching
We are said to be endowed with the opportunity
Of being in a central country.

One who has irreversible actions
Is never inclined to the teaching.
Because we respect and pursue the teaching
Our actions are not irreversible;
Please cultivate only virtue.

Having attained conviction in the teaching,
Our principal pursuit,

We possess the opportunity of faith.

Of the five opportunities
Related to outer conditions,
Shakyamuni Buddha established the first
By visiting this world.
His sojourn was like the sun
Illuminating a dark continent.

By his million perfect virtues
And forms appropriate to disciples' inclinations
He matured and liberated disciples
Who had the fortune to receive his teachings
And he dispersed the murky ignorance
Of countless sentient beings.

Highest of Buddha's activities were those of speech
By which he fulfilled humankind's hopes.
That his disciples might hear, think,
And meditate on his teachings,
Buddha turned the wheel of the teaching
That revealed the four noble truths.

This being the period of the verbal teaching
We have the third opportunity,
That of meeting with the holy teaching.
But once the teaching abides
We must enter its practice.

The teaching will remain five thousand years,
Composed of ten divisions of five hundred years each,
Divided into four periods of doctrine.
The first three periods,
Abiding for fifteen hundred years each,
Are the "doctrine of effect",
The "doctrine of attainment",
And "the doctrine of the verbal teaching".

The final period of five hundred years
Is called the "doctrine of sign-only"

Because people will adhere to the outer form only.
Presently, we are in the seventh or eighth division.

Although the teaching exists
If no one enters its door of practice,
There can be no benefit —
The sun illuminates all continents,
But does it help the blind person see?

There are correct and incorrect ways
To enter Buddha's teaching:
Wishing to benefit this life alone,
To eradicate illness or madness,
To achieve only happiness in this and future lives,
Or just to escape the miseries
Of this and future lives
Are incorrect motivations.

Such practice is said to be
Wishing to be rid of fearful conditions.
Our actual practice, instead, should
Correspond with Buddha's intent:
To lead others towards
The path to liberation and
The high state of complete omniscience.

Although we may have entered the teaching,
Our practice cannot be correct
Unless we depend on a spiritual teacher,
The final opportunity related to outer conditions.

We must rely on his quintessential instructions
Without which there would be no way to practice
The key realizations of Buddha's teaching.

The lama's precept is definitely required.
As Atisha and other great teachers have said,
"If you do not practice the precepts of the lama,
You will remain separate from the teaching."
For this reason we need the lama.

★ ★ ★

Although we may have
The life of perfect leisure and opportunity
Described above,
We are dominated by the three poisons,
Which lead us counter to actual religious practice.
Thus we can lose leisure
Because of current conditions.

The great Buddhist scholars
Classified eight kinds of humans
Who have lost leisure in that way:
Those disturbed by the five poisons,
The utterly dull,
Persons possessed by devils,
Those who are lazy,
Those always involved in wrongdoing,
Those dominated by others,
Those equating religion with deliverance from fear,
And those who enter religion for personal gain.

Persons dominated by the five poisons[36]
Dislike some, holding them distant
And favor others, holding them close.
Although they wish to actualize the teaching,
They cannot.

Those who are extremely dull
Do not possess the slightest glimmer of wisdom.
Even if they enter the door of the teaching,
How can they understand the words they are taught?

If one is in the thrall of a devilish teacher,
Who teaches wrong views and activities
One will embark upon the wrong path,
Whereby one contradicts both aspects of the teaching —
Verbal exposition and experiential insight.

Even if one strongly desires
To learn Buddha's teaching,
If one submits to laziness' power

And makes no effort,
One cannot practice.

One who does not comprehend karma,
The cause and effect of one's actions,
Although making great effort,
Will be lost
In the great ocean of sin
Wherein there exists no knowledge
Of either of the teaching's two aspects.

A person with no independence
Must be the servant of others.
Although wishing to practice
Others will not allow it.

Those who enter religion
From fear of being harmed by others,
Or to obtain food and clothing
Seem to follow religion but in fact
Have no true religious thought.
Because of their wrong motivation
They tend toward irreligious activities.

Finally there are those seeking religion
To gain wealth and become well-known.
Though they appear to be religious
They are only pretending —
How can they travel the path of liberation
When just thinking of themselves?

The above eight types of human beings
Have no time to accomplish
The practice of Buddha's teaching,
And are thus called "leisureless".

There are also eight types without leisure
Because of their strong biases:
Those with tight bonds,
Those always acting wrongly,

Those with no aversion to cyclic existence,
Beings who have not the slightest faith,
Those always involved in non-virtue,
They who are not inclined to the teaching,
Persons who break their vows,
And those not keeping spiritual obligations.

Those tied by bonds of partiality
To wealth, enjoyment, friends, and relatives
Are distracted by the great exertion
They make for those
And have no time to practice the teaching.

There are those who act wrongly
Out of a depraved nature.
The great scholars have said,
"One can rectify disciples' deeds,
But in no way alter their character."
Such persons may meet a spiritual teacher,
But it is difficult for them to turn
Onto the holy teaching's path.

Renunciation is the basis
For entering the religious life.
If one has no fear of
The suffering of lower rebirths,
The faults of cyclic existence,
Or even the suffering in this life,
One will not renounce worldly ways.

The fourth type will never reach liberation
Because their lack of faith
In the lama and the teaching
Blocks the way to the teaching's door.

Those who love sin
Cannot control the three doors
Of body, speech, and mind.
Being separate from knowledge of the teaching
They act only in opposition to it.·

If you offer the teaching
To those in whom there is no light
Of the teaching or any virtuous qualities,
They show no interest;
It is like putting grass before a hungry dog.
Thus they can never generate
The good qualities the teaching provides.

If one enters the teachings
Common to both the Hinayana and Mahayana,
Generates the altruistic aspiration for enlightenment,
And then breaks one's vows,
One will find no place
Except in lower rebirths.
Thus one does not escape a state without leisure.

Persons who enter Secret Mantra
And do not keep their pledges
To lama and spiritual friends
Ruin the purposes of themselves and others
And thus sacrifice any opportunity
For spiritual attainment.

As these eight persons
Are far from the holy teaching
And have shut out
The light of liberation,
They too are known as having no leisure.

When persons do not guard from
These sixteen types of non-leisure
They have only a semblance of religious practice
And of a life of leisure and opportunity.
During this degenerate age
They may imitate a great lama
By sitting on a high throne
Under an ornate umbrella,
Or they may boast of practicing devotion
In a high mountain retreat

Far from worldly activities,
But they are only under the influence
Of some of the sixteen types of non-leisure.
Thus they may appear to practice the teaching
But do not even approach
The actual path to liberation.

★ ★ ★

We should contemplate whether we have
All aspects of leisure and opportunity.
If you have them all
Take joy in this blessing.
Reflect, "Now that I have attained
This life of leisure and opportunity,
I will not waste my time
But will engage in actual practice
No matter what may happen."
Contemplate this again and again.

Even if we are not endowed
With complete leisure and opportunity
We must make great effort
In the various methods of completing them.
We must strive for this
Steadily and continually.

If we lack even one of the aspects
Of leisure and opportunity,
There is no way actually to practice the teaching
And attain the final goal.
When the fulfillment of even a simple worldly task
Requires a combination
Of many causes and conditions,
How much more so the achievement of the final goal!

Even rarer than the conditions for leisure
Are the conditions for opportunity.
Among the requirements for a religious life
One may have just the three
Opportunities related with the self:

To be born human,
In a central country,
With sense organs intact.
For, if one has committed
Irreversible actions
And thus has no faith
In Buddha's teaching,
One is left with only those three aspects.
From among the final two aspects,
Freedom from irreversible actions
Is rare
For we are involved in non-virtuous deeds
Of body, speech, and mind, and
Our actions are motivated
By concern for this life.
Thus one may even be greatly revered
As a scholar and holy man
And yet still possess irreversible karmic actions.

As to the five opportunities
Related with outer conditions,
It is said that though a Buddha visits,
Speaks his teaching,
And his teaching abides,
If no one enters the teaching's door
Only three opportunities can exist.

To enter the door of the teaching
Is not just to request the teaching
Or just to listen to it.
To rightly enter the teaching
One must produce a non-artificial
Mind of renunciation
By realizing that cyclic existence
Is without essence,
Or produce the superior aspiration for enlightenment,
The non-artificial entrance to the Mahayana,
Or at least have the faith of conviction

In the precious Three Jewels.

If one does not have even the latter
One can recite the teaching from memory
Or wear monk's robes
But still not have truly entered the teaching.
Therefore, it is most important
To examine without error
The nature of leisure and opportunity
Just as has been described.

5 The Practice of Going for Refuge

The *Commentary on (Ḏzong-ka-ḇa's) "Foundation of All Excellence"* says:

> *In general life in cyclic existence is only suffering. In particular the suffering of the beings in the unfortunate states is great. We must become greatly afraid of this misery and seek a method to escape it. Generating strong faith in the ability of the Three Jewels to rescue us, we must go for refuge to them.*

Since beginningless time we have repeatedly undergone the suffering of cyclic existence.[37] Having now acquired a perfect human life, if we do not strive to practice virtue immediately, we will again be reborn in lower realms. We must not fail to take advantage of this opportunity to attain Buddhahood. Shantideva says in his *Engaging in the Bodhisattva Deeds*:

> The force of virtue is always weak
> Whereas the force of wrongdoing is great
> And its effects hard to bear.

Therefore, for the most part, our actions cause us to be reborn in lower realms.

Aryadeva says in his *Treatise of Four Hundred Stanzas* (*bzhi brgya pa, catuḥśataka*):

> Having independence and a fit human body,
> If we do not make good use of it
> We will fall into lower realms, be controlled by
>   others,
> And have no way to attain a better life.

We now stand on the boundary between lower and higher states, with the liberty to choose our future happiness or misery. We must make a firm decision to gain happiness. Yet, though we want happiness, we do not have the power to attain it by our own unaided efforts. It is only through the Three Jewels — Buddha, his Teaching, and the Spiritual Community — that we can attain happiness. Therefore, we must rely completely on the Three Jewels with the confidence that, whatever may happen, they will help us. Dignaga says:

> Adrift in the bottomless ocean of cyclic existence,
> Being devoured by the powerful monsters
> Of attachment, hatred, and the other passions —
> To whom should I turn for refuge?

Aryashura replies to this question:

> To the one in whom no fault
> Can ever exist,
> The one in whom all knowledge
> Always exists.

> Those who are sensible
> Go for refuge only to Buddha.
> It is correct to praise and respect him
> And enter into his teaching.

HOW TO GO FOR REFUGE
Identifying the Objects of Refuge
Although Hearers, Self-Enlightened Ones, and Bodhisat-

tvas are all able to help us, it is not sufficient to go to them for ultimate refuge. In order to attain highest liberation, we must go for refuge to all Three Jewels. As is said in the works of the Ḡa-dam-ḃa lamas:

> There are three requisites for travelling from Tibet to India: a guide to show the way, the guide's advice, and companions for assistance. Similarly, we need to rely on Buddha to teach us, the Teaching to show the path, and the Spiritual Community to help us in practicing the Teaching. Again, to cure an illness we need a good doctor, appropriate medicine, and nurses to attend us. One of these alone is not enough; all three are needed. Likewise, in order to attain the highest liberation that eradicates the mental disease of the afflictions, we must depend upon Buddha as the Teacher who shows us the way to liberation, the Teaching, which provides the actual method, and the Spiritual Community which assists us in practicing the Teaching.

The Meaning of Refuge

It is not enough just to recite the refuge prayer; we must find out the actual meaning of refuge. Going for refuge is a mental state composed of either wisdom or a virtuous attitude such as faith, effort, or mindfulness. Going for refuge means that one understands the qualifications and classifications of the Three Jewels, and confidently makes a commitment to them such that one does not call on others for final refuge. One desires to practice the Buddha's teaching and join his followers.

As Ḋzong-ka-ḃa says in his *Great Exposition of the Stages of the Path*:

> The fourfold way of going for refuge includes understanding the classifications of the Three Jewels, understanding their qualifications, committing ourselves to them, and not calling on others for refuge.

Understanding the Qualifications of the Three Jewels

The qualifications of Buddha are understood by contemplating the good qualities of his body, speech, and mind. An Indian teacher praised the qualities of Buddha's body as follows:

> Your body adorned with all its signs
> Is beauty amazing to behold —
> Like a cloudless autumn sky
> Decorated by clusters of stars.

The qualities of Buddha's speech are equally wondrous. When questions are asked by sentient beings of different aspirations, who are so numerous that they fill the sky, Buddha understands them all simultaneously in an instant. He then answers all their questions with a single word, which each being understands according to his or her own capacity. This ability first to cut through each being's net of doubt and ignorance and then to produce correct realization in each according to his or her own capacity for comprehension is the highest method of helping others.

A quality of Buddha's mind is that he directly and simultaneously apprehends both conventional and ultimate truths. Furthermore, because of his great compassion his thoughts are directed solely to the good of others. He never fails in anything he undertakes and always acts at the proper time.

Some skeptic might ask, "How can you say Buddha is helping others when there are still so many people worrying and suffering? Why has he not extended his compassion to these people? Why are they not free from their misery? In order to deliver ourselves from suffering, we need certain inner and outer conditions. Though Buddha has already provided the outer conditions, namely, the Three Jewels, we ourselves do not fulfill the complete inner condition of faith and therefore remain subject to suffering. As Ashvaghosha said in his praise of Buddha called the *Hundred Fifty Verses of Praise* (*brgya lgna bcu pa zhes bya ba'i bstod pa, śatapañcāśatkanāmastotra*):

> You, Lord, have fully provided
> The powerful outer conditions.
> Because all the inner conditions are not present
> Ordinary persons remain subject to suffering.

For instance, the sun always shines. If a cave facing north or a blind man does not receive its light, this is not due to a deficiency on the part of the sun but rather to their own situation. Like the sun, Buddha, without partiality, ceaselessly radiates the rays of his blessings. If sentient beings remain in bondage to suffering, it is because their inner state is not sufficiently receptive.

Once we reach a clear understanding of Buddha's qualifications, we will see how skillfully he has communicated the eighty-four thousand aggregates of his teaching. These vary according to their definitive meaning, the capacities of the listeners, and the effects they are intended to produce. That Buddha taught from these three points of view further reveals his qualifications.

Briefly, we can understand that Buddha is a suitable object of refuge by considering his wisdom, compassion, and ability. These manifest in the following four ways. Buddha is:

1 free from all fear of suffering
2 skilled in the method of delivering others from their fear
3 impartial towards everyone
4 engaged in work for the welfare of all, whether they are helpful or harmful to him.

Once we understand Buddha's qualifications, we will realize that they arise from his practice of the Teaching, and this will produce respect for the Teaching. As the Spiritual Community is made up of those who correctly practice the Teaching, we will have respect for the members of the Spiritual Community as well. To more fully understand Buddha's qualifications we should refer to the reasoning provided by Dharmakirti in his *Precise Commentary* (see chapter two, above).

Understanding the Six Classifications of the Three Jewels
The Three Jewels, the objects of refuge, can be classified in six ways, each of which provides a basis for going for refuge. We can go for refuge by classifying the Three Jewels:

1 according to their definitions: Buddha is the fully enlightened one; the Teaching is virtue in the beginning, middle, and end; and the members of the Spiritual Community are those who actually attain the path through relying on the instructions of others.
2 according to their activities: Buddha helps by giving the verbal Teaching; the Teaching helps by giving the realization that eradicates mental and physical suffering, and the Spiritual Community helps by rejoicing at others' virtues.
3 according to our faith: by thinking, "I will pay homage to Buddha, I will actualize the Teaching, and I will join with the Spiritual Community."
4 according to our practice: by thinking, "I will pay homage to Buddha, I will meditate on the Teaching, and I will share both material and spiritual enjoyments with the Spiritual Community."
5 according to our recollection of their qualifications.
6 according to their power as fields of merit which increase our merit through obeisance, offerings, and other forms of worship.

Commitment to the Three Jewels
Once we commit ourselves wholeheartedly to Buddha as the right person to teach us the method of protection from suffering, we must follow him as resolutely as one obliged to appear before a fierce ruler would follow the advice of a friend who knows how to placate the ruler. Once we commit ourselves to actualizing the holy Teaching, we must

resolve to practice it, just as one desiring a government position must learn the methods of administration. Once we commit ourselves to joining with the members of the Spiritual Community, we must resolve to follow their example and counsel, just as one desiring to cross the ocean in a ship for the first time would follow the routine of experienced sailors. Since making the above resolutions is of foremost importance in going for refuge, these commitments to each of the Three Jewels are most crucial.

Not Calling On Others For Refuge
After understanding the differences between Buddhist and non-Buddhist teachers, teachings, and spiritual communities, we should go for refuge to the Three Jewels by determining not to accept non-Buddhist teachers as our guides. If we regard the knowledge of a worldly god[38] as superior to that of Buddha and entrust ourselves to that god, we forsake the Three Jewels. However, as long as we do not regard such gods as the equal of Buddha, we may rely upon them in order to accomplish some particular temporal work, just as we rely upon a doctor for help when we are sick.

One non-Buddhist who converted to Buddhism praised Buddha as follows:

> Having abandoned other teachers
> I go for refuge to you, O Lord.
> If you should ask why, I would answer,
> "You have no faults and have all knowledge."

> I have carefully studied
> The scriptures of non-Buddhists —
> When I examine your teachings
> I become faithful to you, O Protector!

> We who have no omniscience
> Are always criticizing others,
> But I found no fault in you.
> You alone are the teacher without fault.

In brief, the instructions for refuge explained here are extremely important to each practitioner of Buddha's Teaching, whether their capacity to practice is small, middling, or great. As Maitreya says in his *Sublime Continuum of the Mahayana* (*rgyud bla ma, mahāyānottaratantraśāstra*):

> Buddha indicated three objects of refuge —
> The Teacher, Teaching, and Spiritual Community —
>
> According to the faith
> Of the followers of the three vehicles.

Gyel-tsap Dar-ma-rin-chen (*rgyal tshab dar ma rin chen*), one of Dzong-ka-ba's two chief disciples, said:

> Once we reach a clear understanding of going for refuge, we will also understand that all the scriptures and their commentaries are factors of having gone for refuge.

All Buddha's teachings are included in the teachings of the stages of the path for the three types of practitioners, those of small, middling, and great capacities. These teachings in turn are included in the practice of going for refuge. Even for persons not engaged in studying the scriptures, the practice of refuge is essential and of great benefit. Such people rely upon the true words of holy persons and go for refuge with great faith, thinking, "Whatever may happen good or bad, you know how to help me."

The practice for a person of small capacity, like ourselves, is precisely the practice of going for refuge in the Three Jewels. This sort of practitioner contemplates the difficulty of attaining a human life endowed with leisure and opportunity, the impermanence of life and imminence of death, and the suffering in lower realms of being. By means of this practice he or she gains unwavering faith in the three objects of refuge as well as a desire to abandon the ten non-virtuous actions.

A person of middling capacity produces unwavering faith in Buddha's teachings on the cause and effect of actions. Consequently, he or she is intent upon turning away from misdeeds and practicing virtuous actions. As this is the essence of going for refuge to the Teaching, the practice of the person of middling capacity is not different from the practice of refuge.

The practitioner of great capacity is motivated only by an altruistic aspiration to attain the highest enlightenment for the sake of others. This, too, is no different from the practice of going for refuge. In this way, all Buddha's teachings are included in the various practices developed for the three types of practitioners, and these practices in turn are included in the practice of going for refuge. Buddha did not discriminate against any of his followers by giving some a higher teaching of refuge and others a lower teaching of refuge. The above distinctions arose according to his followers' own experience of the practice.

Measure of Going For Refuge
In order to define the measure of going for refuge, we must first understand that a refuge is something upon which we can depend: that is, something which, when relied upon, provides an effective support for the elimination of all our faults and problems. Thus, the measure of going for refuge is to possess deep confidence in the objects of refuge, the Three Jewels. When we say, "I go for refuge to Buddha," we should think, "Whatever may happen to me, you, Buddha, know how to help me." When we recite, "I go to refuge to the Teaching," we should firmly resolve to practice the Teaching. When we recite, "I go for refuge to the Spiritual Community," we should determine to learn the practice of the holy Teaching just as do the members of the Spiritual Community.

How The Three Objects of Refuge Protect
If we should suddenly die, which of the three refuges

would be the actual refuge that protects us from misery in future lives? Most of us perhaps would answer that it is Buddha, or our lama, the direct objects of our faith. However, though both the lama and Buddha have great power to protect us from mental and physical suffering, they are not our actual refuge. As Buddha said:

> Buddhas do not wash away sins with water,
> Clear away the suffering of beings with their hands,
> Nor transfer their realization to others.
> They liberate beings by showing them the teaching.

If we fear mental and physical suffering, we search for a method to free ourselves from that suffering. Lamas and Buddhas can teach us such a method; they are the ones who can indicate a true refuge. The members of the Spiritual Community are our friends and helpers who instruct and inspire us. But, among the Three Jewels, the Buddha Jewel and the Spiritual Community Jewel cannot actually protect us. The Teaching Jewel is the actual refuge, but unless we actually practice it ourselves, it will not free us from our fears. We are like sick persons looking for a remedy, Buddha is like a doctor, and the Teaching is like medicine. But if we do not take the medicine the doctor prescribes, we will not be cured.

Once there was a heavenly prince named Shin-du-den-ba (*shin tu brtan pa*), who foresaw with clairvoyance that he would soon die and be reborn in a lower realm. Overcome with fear, he sought refuge with Indra, the king of the worldly gods, who suggested that he visit Buddha and request a method of protection from fear. Thus, Indra acted as a member of the Spiritual Community, assisting him to attain refuge. When Shin-du-den-ba visited Buddha, he was instructed to recite a spiritual formula called "Dzuk dor ñam gyel ma" (*gtsug tor rnam rgyal ma*). Thus Buddha was the teacher of the method of refuge. Shin-du-den-ba then endeavored to recite the words of the formula and succeeded in preventing his rebirth into the lower realms.

In this sense, the teaching was the actual refuge.

The Actual Practice of Refuge For Beginners
Since it is presently impossible for most of us to see Buddha
plainly, we must depend upon the lama, as his representa-
tive, to indicate the teachings. Buddha indicated throughout his teachings that he would from time to time reappear
in the world as an ordinary person in order to liberate living
beings. He is always sending emanations, who often appear
as lamas. Therefore, although our teacher may seem to be
an ordinary person, we can rely upon him as if he were the
actual Buddha.[39]

We should endeavor to go for refuge to the lama and the
Three Jewels with unwavering faith in the following way:
First develop a sense of fear about the misery that follows
death, and then commit yourself to the lama with heartfelt
devotion, thinking, "Whatever happens to me, good or
bad, you, Lama, know what is best. If I must be sick, bless
me to be sick; if I must die, bless me to die." While
reciting, "I go for refuge to the Lama, I go for refuge to
Buddha," contemplate the great kindness of the Lama and
Buddha in showing you the method to free yourself from
suffering. While reciting, "I go for refuge to the Teaching,"
resolve to abandon wrongdoing and cultivate virtue in keeping with your lama's instructions. While reciting, "I go for
refuge to the Spiritual Community," remember the story of
Shin-du-den-ba and feel confident that by reciting the refuge prayer, you also will be liberated from rebirth in lower
realms.

You can also practice going for refuge in the following
way: first clean up the room in which you meditate and
prepare representations of Buddha's body, speech and
mind.[40] Arrange offerings in beautiful order in front of
these representations, and then sit on a comfortable cushion
in the correct meditative posture. After examining your
motivation, think, "Although I have attained a human life,
if I am careless in guarding my mind, I will still accumulate

faults. Then, immediately after my death, I will fall into lower realms where the suffering will be unbearable." In this way you will produce great fear.

Visualize your father on your right side and your mother on your left. Surrounding you, imagine the innumerable sentient beings of the six realms. Realize that all sentient beings are your kind mothers of past and future lives and that they suffer just as you do. Then generate deep compassion for them and think, "I must attain the high state of Buddhahood in order to help all these beings."

Now that you have produced a special virtuous mind, visualize the field of assembly: imagine in the vast sky before you a jewelled throne which is high and wide, supported by eight great lions. Upon it is a cushion that is a mandala of multi-colored lotus, moon, and sun. Seated upon this is your own root lama[41] appearing as Shakyamuni Buddha. His body is the color of purified gold, and he has a crown protuberance upon his head. His right hand is touching the earth, and his left is in the gesture of meditative equipoise; upon it is a begging bowl filled with the nectar of blessings. His body is beautifully covered with the three saffron colored religious robes of a monk. He sits cross-legged in the middle of an aura of light. In his heart is Vajradhara Buddha, and in Vajradhara's heart is a blue "*hūṃ*" radiating light.

Behind Shakyamuni Buddha is another lion throne with a cushion of lotus, moon, and sun, upon which Vajradhara is seated, surrounded by lamas belonging to the lineage of the blessings of practice. On Shakyamuni Buddha's right is Maitreya, surrounded by lamas in the lineage of extensive deeds, and on his left is Manjushri, surrounded by lamas in the lineage of profound view. In front of Shakyamuni Buddha sits your gracious root lama just as you see him when receiving his teachings. He is surrounded by the lamas with whom you have a religious connection — those in direct lineage from Buddha down to your own root lama. Encircling them are, first, the assemblies of tutelary deities, and then, in turn, the Buddhas, Bodhisattvas, Self-Enlightened Ones, Hearers, heroes, heroines, protectors of the teaching, and other wisdom deities. In front of each, on a jewelled stand, their own religious teachings appear as volumes of scripture whose nature is light. Inconceivable manifestations of each of the assembly radiate to the ten directions, subduing all sentient beings according to their capacities. Envision that the entire assembly is gazing at you with great joy.

Then think:

> I and all sentient beings, fearing the suffering of cyclic existence and seeing the qualifications of the Three Jewels, recite with one voice:
>
> > I go for refuge to the holy glorious lamas —
> > The gracious root lama and the lamas of the
> >   lineage —
> > Essence of all the activities and good
> >   qualities
> > Of body, speech and mind of all the
> >   Buddhas
> > Of the ten directions and three times,[42]
> > Source of the eighty-four thousand
> >   aggregates of the teaching,
> > Those who possess the entire Spiritual
> >   Community.

Recite:

> I go for refuge to the Lama.

Sincerely reciting this prayer many times causes streams of nectar to flow forth from the bodies of your lama, both in his usual form and in the form of Shakyamuni Buddha, as well as from the lamas of both direct and indirect lineages. As these streams enter the bodies and minds of yourself and all other living beings, they purify everyone from all defilements of wrongdoing, transgressions, and ills in general. In particular, they purify everyone from all wrong done while depending on the lama, for example, proudly comparing one's own body with that of the lama, being inattentive to his speech, and disturbing his mind. As this purification takes place, your own and others' bodies are transformed into pure, clear light, and everyone's merit, lifespan, and knowledge of both aspects of the Teaching — verbal exposition and experiential insight — are increased and extended. After considering that the blessings from the body, speech, and mind of the lama have entered you and all the others, think:

We have come under the protection of the Lama.

Next recite:

I go for refuge to the Buddha.

Sincerely reciting this prayer many times causes streams of nectar to flow forth from the bodies of all the Buddhas including Vajradhara and others. As these streams enter the bodies and minds of yourself and all other beings, they purify everyone from all defilements of wrongdoing in general. In particular, they purify everyone from the defilements of wrongdoing created with regard to Buddha, such as causing blood to flow from Buddha's body through harmful thoughts, making a livelihood by selling Buddha images, finding bad qualities in Buddha, and destroying temples and memorials of enlightenment. After considering that the blessings of the body, speech, and mind of the Buddhas have entered you and all others, think:

We have come under the protection of the Buddhas.

Then recite:

I go for refuge to the Teaching.

Sincerely reciting this prayer many times causes streams of nectar to flow forth from the scriptures. As these streams enter the bodies and minds of yourself and all others, they purify everyone from all defilements of wrongdoing in general. In particular, they purify everyone from all the defilements of wrongdoing created with regard to the Teaching. These include such non-virtuous actions as despising or abandoning the Teaching — for example selling or pawning scriptures, placing them uncovered on the ground, and stepping over or upon them. These nectar streams further purify everyone especially from the defilements of despising the Teaching and its promoters and of obstructing speakers and devotees. After considering that the blessings of the Teaching have entered you and all others, think:

> We have come under the protection of the Teaching.

Then recite:

> I go for refuge to the Spiritual Community.

Sincerely reciting this prayer many times causes streams of nectar to flow forth from the bodies of the assemblage of wisdom beings — protectors of the Teaching, heroes, heroines, Self-Enlightened Ones, Hearers, and Bodhisattvas. As these streams enter the bodies and minds of yourself and all others, they purify everyone from all the defilements of wrongdoing in general. In particular, they purify you and all others from wrongdoing accumulated with regard to the Spiritual Community, such as causing dissension in the Spiritual Community, using its property, and slandering its members. After considering that the blessings of the Spiritual Community have entered you and all others, think:

> We have all come under the protection of the Spiritual Community.

To specifically go for refuge to the tutelary deities and to the protectors of the teaching, say the following prayer:

> I go for refuge to the tutelary deities and the gods of the mandala, along with their heavenly attendants.

Sincerely reciting this prayer many times causes streams of

nectar to flow forth from the bodies of the deities. As these streams enter the bodies and minds of yourself and all beings, they purify you of transgressing or corrupting both the basic and accessory promises made in the general vows offered to the five Buddha lineages. They also purify you of transgression or corruption with respect to particular vows offered to other deities. After considering that the blessings of the deities have entered you and all others, think:

> We are all suitable vessels to generate the special realizations of the two stages of the Vajrayana.

Then recite:

> I go for refuge to the holy, glorious protectors, those who have the eye of transcendent wisdom, guardians who protect the teaching.

Sincerely reciting this prayer many times causes a brilliant flame-like light to emanate from the bodies of the protectors, including Mahakala and others. As this light enters your body, it burns away all madness, sickness, and defilements of wrongdoing, destroying them completely. After considering that the blessings of the protectors have entered your body and mind, think firmly:

> I have come under the protection of the great protectors, and no longer have the capacity for any sickness, madness, or any other obstacle.[43]

All the objects of refuge then say, "We are your protectors, refuge and allies, ready to deliver you from the suffering of cyclic existence." As they recite this clearly, promising to help you, rejoice. Thus, with deep prayer, and with tears pouring forth from your eyes and the hairs of your body standing on end, go for refuge.

After you have gone for refuge to each being individually in this way, go for refuge to all together, conjoining it with generation of the altruistic aspiration for enlightenment. Just as a warrior in a fierce battle wishes to protect not only himself, but also his relatives and friends, so you should chiefly think of the needs of sentient beings. Recite:

> I go for refuge until enlightenment
> To Buddha, the Teaching, and the Spiritual
>   Community.

Sincerely reciting this prayer many times causes streams of nectar to flow forth from the bodies of all the members of the field of assembly. As these streams enter the bodies and minds of yourself and all others and purify everyone from all defilements of wrongdoing, the bodies of all are transformed into pure, clear light. All merit, lifespan, and all the knowledge of both aspects of the teaching are expanded and increased in everyone. Think:

> The blessings of the Three Jewels have entered myself and all others.

Then recite:

> By the merit of practicing the six perfections
> May I achieve Buddhahood in order to help living
>   beings.

Recite this many times and meditate deeply on generating the altruistic aspiration for enlightenment. A duplicate form of Shakyamuni Buddha enters your body and you become Shakyamuni Buddha. Rays of light emanate from your transformed body and strike all sentient beings who have all been your mother and father, purifying them of their defilements and alleviating their suffering. Think:

> I am establishing them in the high state of Shakyamuni Buddha.

This is the way to generate the altruistic aspiration for enlightenment in order to formalize the path and final goal for others.

Then recite:

> I go for refuge to the Three Jewels.

I confess each and every misdeed.
I rejoice in the virtue of living beings.
I hold in my mind the thought of enlightenment
   and the Buddha.

To Buddha, the Teaching, and the Spiritual
   Community
I go for refuge until enlightenment.
In order to fully accomplish the purposes of others
I will generate the aspiration for enlightenment.

After generating this superior aspiration
I will cherish all sentient beings
And perform the beautiful, highest deeds of
   enlightenment.
May I achieve Buddhahood to help sentient beings.

As you recite this prayer from the *Tantra of the Dakinis'*
Vajra Song (*mkha' 'gro ma rdo rje gur gyi rgyud*), contemplate
the following:

> Going for refuge is the basis for everything, just as
> the earth is the foundation for all existence. Confes-
> sing wrongdoing is like clearing away rocks and
> weeds from a field. Rejoicing at others' virtue is like
> the water and other cooperative causes that assist
> growth. Generating the altruistic aspiration for en-
> lightenment is the seed. By producing the crops of
> Bodhisattva-deeds, all beings will be sustained.

The cultivation of the four immeasurables[44] increases the
aim and scope of the altruistic aspiration for enlightenment.
The thought of benefiting all sentient beings, which is
central to the generation of the aspiration for enlightenment, is simply the intention to remove their sufferings and
promote their happiness. The wish to clear away their suffering is *compassion,* and the wish to establish them in
happiness is *loving-kindness.* Because the defiled happiness
of worldly enjoyments is deceptive and unreliable, you
should aim to establish beings in the indestructible unde-

filed happiness of liberation. *Joy* is delight in others' attainment of the undefiled happiness of liberation. It must be accompanied by *equanimity,* an impartial attitude towards friends, enemies, and beings towards whom you feel indifferent.

The four immeasurables are cultivated through four basic reflections. To cultivate loving-kindness, reflect:

> From beginningless time all sentient beings, my mothers, have wished only for happiness. However, they have not created any causes of happiness or found any opportunity to enjoy true, lasting happiness. Whatever defiled happiness they have gained has turned into suffering. How good it would be if they could enjoy happiness and create the causes of happiness. May this come to pass.

To cultivate compassion, think:

> From beginningless time these beings created only causes of suffering and are now undergoing immeasurable pain. Moreover, even now they are producing the causes of future misery. How good it would be if they were free from suffering and the causes of suffering. May they be free from suffering.

To cultivate joy, think:

> How good it would be if these beings were inseparable from happiness that is free from suffering. May they be inseparable from it.

To cultivate equanimity, reflect:

> Since beginningless time these beings have discriminated between friends and enemies, favoring the former and hating the latter. Under the influence of attachment and aversion they have committed various misdeeds, and as a consequence have experienced the immeasurable sufferings of the lower

realms. How good it would be if these beings could abide in equanimity, free from the bias of attachment and aversion. I, too, will develop equanimity toward all, without discrimination between friends and enemies.

After you have thus visualized the objects of equanimity, recite the prayer for the four immeasurables:[45]

> May all sentient beings enjoy happiness and the causes of happiness.
> May all sentient beings be freed from suffering and the causes of suffering.
> May all sentient beings be inseparable from happiness that is free from suffering.
> May all sentient beings abide in equanimity, free from attachment and aversion.

Sincerely reciting this prayer many times causes immeasurable streams of nectar to flow forth from the bodies of all the members of the field of assembly. As these streams enter all sentient beings, they purify all their actions, afflictive emotions, obstructions, and wrongdoing, such as attachment and aversion and the mental and physical sufferings caused by them. Think:

> May they abide in the four immeasurables and attain perfect, undefiled happiness.

Motivated by faith conjoined with reflective meditation on the extensive and profound paths, recite the salutation from Nagarjuna's *Treatise on the Middle Way* (*dbu ma'i bstan bcos, mūlamadhyamakakārikā*).[46] When you wish to offer ablutions, imagine a bathing chamber and invite the field of assembly there. Visualize gods bringing vessels filled with nectar for the ablutions. Offer them along with heavenly robes and ornaments. If you wish, you can recite the extensive prayer of the seven aspects of worship, and offer the mandala. Then recite either the "Foundation of All Excellence" or the "Three Great Purposes".[47]

At the end of the session, envision a ray of light radiating from Shakyamuni Buddha's heart and entering the entire assembly. All dissolve into light, which is absorbed into Shakyamuni Buddha. Shakyamuni Buddha then melts into the space between your two eyebrows. Imagine that you have received the blessings of all the field of assembly. Then recite a deep prayer of aspiration and dedication of merit.

Like sick persons who take whatever medicine is necessary to cure their illness, we must strive to go for refuge to cure the illness of our suffering. As Shantideva says in his *Engaging in the Bodhisattva Deeds*:

> For even a common illness
> One must follow the doctor's advice.
> What need be said of the constant infection
> Of desire, hatred, and ignorance,
> Origins of so many ills.

Since Buddha has prescribed the medicine that cures the mental illness with which we have been afflicted since beginningless time, it is most crucial that we go for refuge to him. Persons on their deathbeds must go immediately for refuge with great faith, for they cannot put it off until tomorrow. Likewise, we too must go for refuge right now. The practice of going for refuge is not an insignificant teaching; it is stated in many sutras and commentaries that if we fear suffering after death and go for refuge, this is as profound as the practice of the Vajrayana's development and fulfillment stages. Once we practice going for refuge to the lama and the Three Jewels until it becomes spontaneous, it will benefit us in both this and future lives. Once we have this kind of faith, we will then automatically remember the lama and the Three Jewels at the moment of death and never be harmed by suffering especially by rebirth in the lower realms.

The good qualities of faith are immeasurable. As Buddha states in the *Precious Lamp Sutra* (*dkon mchog ta la la, ratnolkāsūtra*):

> Faith is the prerequisite of all virtue,
> A procreator giving birth like a mother.
> It nurtures and increases all excellence,
> Clears away doubts, rescues from the four rivers,[48]
> And is a prosperous city of happiness.

> Faith clarifies our minds, eradicates pride,
> And is the root of respect.
> It is great wealth and a treasure.
> Like hands, it is the means of gathering virtue.
> Like feet, it is the means of travelling the path.

The Precepts of Going for Refuge

These precepts prohibit some actions and enjoin others. Once we follow the proscriptive precepts, we will be protected by the Three Jewels, for we will be relying upon our conviction in the cause and effect of karma.

One of the principal precepts of going for refuge is the injunction to rely upon a spiritual teacher. Although Buddha is not manifestly present before us now, our spiritual teacher, our lama, represents him. Our lama is the one who indicates refuge to us, and our faith in him is in itself a refuge. Thus it is most essential to rely upon the lama. Avoid those who are not faithful to their lama, for by keeping company with them your own faith will be defiled. Once we rely upon a lama, whatever work we choose to undertake will be accomplished. Therefore, praying to worldly gods is a sign that we lack faith in our lama and the Three Jewels.

Always offer the first portion of your food or drink to the Three Jewels. Of course, the Three Jewels do not need the food, but through this action you will never lack food and drink.

It is said we should go for refuge three times during the day and three times at night. However, it is sufficient to do so just once at any time, though in the morning is best.

The Benefits of Going for Refuge
Because the benefits of going for refuge are too many to
enumerate fully, we will here mention only the eight principal benefits. Once we have gone for refuge to Buddha, his
Teaching, and his Spiritual Community:

1 we can call ourselves Buddhists
2 we will be fit to take pure vows
3 our wrongdoing will decrease
4 we will accumulate vast merit
5 we will not be reborn in a lower realm
6 neither humans nor non-humans will harm us
7 all our good wishes will be fulfilled
8 we will quickly attain Buddhahood.

Moreover, the practice of going for refuge to the lama and
the Three Jewels is the best way to ransom off the Lord of
Death, thereby prolonging our lives. As Nga-wang-drak-ba
says in his *Quintessential Instructions on Ransoming off Death*
(*'chi ba blu ba'i man ngag*):

> Those striving to pay ransom to death's lord
> Can pay it by means of faith.

The following story illustrates how the practice of going for
refuge protects us against harm from humans and non-
humans. There was once an old monk who received from a
donor a piece of fine quality cotton cloth. A thief noticed
the gift and followed the monk to his home. That night, the
thief knocked on the monk's door and demanded, "I need
that piece of cloth you received today." Realizing that there
was no way out, the old monk replied, "Certainly you may
have my cloth, but I am afraid to see you. I received this gift
from my donor today with my own two hands. Please
extend yours through the opening in my door and I will give
you the material." When the thief put both hands through
the opening, the monk bound them together with a rope.
Stepping outside, he then recited, "I go for refuge to Buddha; I go for refuge to the Teaching; I go for refuge to the

Spiritual Community," all the while thrashing the thief with a stick. The thief thought, "I am glad there are no more than three objects of refuge. If there were more I would soon die." With this thought, his faith in the Three Jewels was awakened. Thereafter he continually recited this refuge prayer, gave up his evil livelihood, and took the vows of a lay practitioner.

Now this layman was accustomed to sleeping under a bridge over which many demons would pass, but after he had begun his practice of going for refuge the demons no longer used the bridge. To that place came an evil heretic who owned a magical rope which he used in order to catch whatever he desired, but when he commanded the rope to catch the layman, it would not respond. The heretic approached the laymen and asked what power he possessed to perform such a feat. The layman replied, "I know nothing more than how to recite the prayer of going for refuge to the Three Jewels." This alone had the power to protect him.

6 The Cause and Effect of Actions

The *Commentary on (Ḏzong-ka-ḇa's) "Foundation of All Excellence"* says:

> *After we have gone for refuge to the Three Jewels, it is very important to produce faith in the law of the cause and effect of actions (karma), for this is the root of all well-being. Regarding this law, Buddha gave the following general teaching in the* Sutra on the Many Kinds of Actions *(mdo sde las brgya ba):*
>
> > *The actions of embodied beings*
> > *Will never be lost in even one hundred aeons —*
> > *They will simply give their effects*
> > *When their conditions and time arise.*

Buddha said in the Great Nirvana Sutra *(mya ngan las 'das pa chen po'i mdo, mahāparinirvāṇasūtra):*

> > *Those who always want happiness*
> > *For themselves and others do no wrong.*
> > *When the childlike who desire happiness*
> > *Do wrong, they must suffer the results.*

THE TEN NON-VIRTUOUS ACTIONS[49]

The great scholars have written that
The significance of teaching
The cause and effect of actions
Is that we discard non-virtuous actions
And adopt virtuous ones.

There are only two kinds of rebirth —
Fortunate and unfortunate.
We must analyze our virtuous and non-virtuous deeds
For these alone create such rebirths;
We do not end up there by chance.
"Strive to abandon non-virtue,
And cultivate virtue," the great teachers exhort.

Non-virtuous activities are ten:
Taking the lives of sentient beings,
Taking things not given,
And sexual misconduct
Are the three physical non-virtues.

Lying, slander, harsh, and idle speech
Are the four verbal non-virtues.

Covetousness, harmful thought, and wrong views
Are the mental non-virtues.

To explain a little further,
Killing may be motivated
By hatred, attachment, or ignorance.
Among all killing
That of parents and Arhats
Are heinous sins. It is said
For such killers, there is no bardo,
Just immediate rebirth
In unfortunate states.

A complete act of killing
Has four components:

Object, motive, activity, and completion.
The object is any sentient being;
The motive, the thought to kill;
The activity, to carry out the slaying;
The completion, the being's death.
But humans kill for no reason.
To see human killing human
In so many different ways
Breaks the hearts
Of those with compassion.

Stealing means to take without permission.
Its three types are
To take by force, concealment, or deceit.
Stealing by force includes not only robbers,
But soldiers and terrorists as well.
Concealment is taking without the owner's knowledge,
Deceit, by using false pretenses.

Sexual misconduct differs
For laymen and monks.
If this non-virtuous action
Is prohibited for even laymen,
What need mention monks
Who have the vow of liberation?
This is a grave non-virtue
Because it is a great cause
Of breaking one's vows.
Monks must be especially careful.
Those who have the lay vow of upavasa
Must abstain on their special days.
Sex with the sick
Is forbidden to all.

The three kinds of lies are
Ordinary, great, and spiritual lies.
Speaking falsely to deceive others
Is called an ordinary lie.
Deceiving others with non-Buddhist statements

Is called a great lie — for example,
That virtue brings no benefit,
That non-virtue brings no suffering,
That paradise is not blissful —
For nothing more false can be said.

A spiritual lie is to claim
Attainment of path stages
Not yet attained.
Some claim clairvoyance,
Seeing future and past.
Clairvoyance can be sullied or pure;
Do not rely on those with the former
For they are sometimes right, sometimes wrong.
Only holy beings' clairvoyance is pure,
But it is never found in an ordinary person.
Those who say that they have seen
A god or devil
In order to deceive others
Are also telling spiritual lies.
The great scholars taught the importance
Of not trusting such deceit,
And of properly distinguishing the truth.

Slander may be open or concealed.
When, in the presence of two friends
A third and powerful person
Accuses one of having harmed the other,
He or she is guilty of open slander.
Talking privately to one or the other
In order to divide the two
Is called concealed slander.

The gravest of these
Is causing dissension
Among Buddha's followers
Or between teacher and disciple.
Dividing husband and wife or close friends
Is another serious non-virtue.

To call another "ugly"
Even if not beautiful
Or to mock as "blind" the sightless
Or the lame as "crippled"
And any such talk of others' faults
Even if spoken sweetly
Is considered harsh speech
If it makes them unhappy.

The brahmins of India have mantras
That destroy their enemies;
Claiming this as religious work
Is called idle speech.
Singing songs with desire,
Talking about armies, robbers, and so on,
If it only summons up desire and hatred
Then it too is idle,
Serving only to distract.
We should recite prayers instead.

Covetousness is greed
For others' possessions:
"How nice to have that myself!"
This desire produces schemes
For obtaining others' wealth.

Harmful thought is a malicious wish,
Such as, "I want to cause trouble,"
Or, disliking others' wealth, to think,
"How nice if they should lose their fortune,"
Or to be pleased at another's adversity —
All these exemplify a harmful mind.
Any harmful act at all
Is classed as this non-virtue.

Wrong views include
Belief that actions yield no effects,
Or that wrongdoing is irreproachable,
And adherence to either one

Of the two extreme views —
Nihilism and eternalism.
All views
Negating cause and effect of actions
Are wrong views.
The commentaries enumerate many
Non-Buddhist ideas, but in brief form
They are either nihilist or eternalist.

Eternalists believe
The self is a permanent entity,
That the world is created
By a permanent deity
Like Vishnu or Maheshvara.

Nihilists do not accept a creator,
Saying no one made
The rising of the sun,
The flowing down of water,
The roundness of beans,
The sharpness of thorns,
The beautiful hues
In the peacock's plumage.
Nihilists say that these things,
Never having been created,
Are just self-generated.
Since nothing has causes
Former and future lives do not exist,
Nor have actions any effect;
Thus there is no liberation.
To understand their views,
Investigate their treatises.

Wrong views and killing are gravest
Among the ten non-virtues.
That killing is serious
Is easy to see,
But why so wrong views?
Because one who so holds

Cannot accept Buddha's word
Nor take any vows.
Once influenced by wrong ideas,
Even cultivating virtue
Will not lead to liberation.
Confession does not help
When a person lacks faith.

These are the ten non-virtues.
Abandoning them
One naturally engages in virtue.

A god once asked Buddha a question in verse:

> Which are sharp weapons?
> Which virulent poison?
> Which a blazing fire?
> And which great darkness?

Buddha replied:

> Poisonous words are sharp weapons;
> Desire, the virulent poison;
> Hatred, a blazing fire;
> And ignorance, the great darkness.

It is also said in scripture:

> There is no swamp like desire,
> And no harm like hatred.
> Nothing is more extensive than ignorance,
> There is no river like craving.

Once one has understood well the faults of cyclic existence — especially through contemplating impermanence and the cause and effect of actions — a practitioner generates the desire to be liberated from this type of existence.

7 Desire For Liberation

The *Commentary on (Ḏzong-ka-ɓa's) "Foundation of All Excellence"* says:

> By making effort, beginning with mindfulness of death and continuing through the cultivation of right actions and the rejection of wrong, we will attain rebirth as a fortunate being. Yet, at this stage, we are still tightly bound by actions and afflictive emotions, and in the future we will certainly fall back into the lower states of unfortunate beings. In the prison of the three realms of cyclic existence, we will continue to be tortured on the rack of the three kinds of suffering. Therefore, we must produce the desire for release and then travel the path to liberation. Concerning the former, Ḏzong-ka-ɓa says in the Foundation of all Excellence (*you tan gzhir gyur ma*):
>
>> The door to all misery is our dissatisfaction
>> with enjoyments.
>> Having realized the ills of worldly marvels,
>> Which offer us no security,
>> May I be strongly intent on the bliss of
>> liberation. (v.5)

Just as a mother cares for her children, Buddha came to this world in order to free all sentient beings from the sufferings of cyclic existence.[50] Such liberation from the bondage of cyclic existence is known as freedom. Before one can develop a desire for liberation, it is necessary first to understand the disadvantages of the suffering that characterizes all cyclic existence and then the causal process by which one enters cyclic existence.

In order to help sentient beings understand this, Buddha's first discourse was an explanation of the four noble truths. Just as a desire to quell the suffering of thirst depends upon one's not wanting to be tormented by thirst, so the desire for liberation from cyclic existence depends upon one's not wanting to be tormented by the suffering experienced there. Therefore, even though chronologically the causes of suffering come before suffering, Buddha taught the truth of suffering first and the causes of suffering second: "Bhikshus, this is the noble truth of suffering. This is the noble truth of suffering's cause."

The sequence of this teaching accords with the stages of practice. Thus, it is very significant that Buddha taught the first two truths in a sequence different from their actual order of arising. For, in the beginning disciples were defiled by the darkness of ignorance and erroneously thought of the world — which is actually a place of suffering — as something to be enjoyed. Unless they first generated the root of liberation, an unmistaken desire to be liberated from cyclic existence, Buddha could not lead them. Therefore, Buddha initially taught the truth of suffering. For, after being taught the varieties of suffering, one will generate an aversion to them.

Then, once his listeners understood the way in which they were sunk into an ocean of suffering and wished to be liberated from it, they understood the necessity for overcoming suffering and recognized that this cannot be done unless one overcomes the causes of suffering. Hence the teaching on the truth of suffering leads one to contemplate what might be the cause of that suffering. For this reason, Buddha next taught the truth of the causes of suffering. These can be understood in accordance with Buddha's teaching: "The suffering of cyclic existence is caused by contaminated actions; these actions are caused by the afflictive emotions. The root cause of these, in turn, should be understood as the conception of an inherently existent self."

Once one understands that this conception of self can be overcome, one sees that it is definitely possible to actualize a cessation of suffering. In order to make this clear, Buddha next taught the truth of the cessation of suffering. Someone might think that Buddha could have made this the second truth because, once the disciples had heard about the truth of suffering and generated a desire to be liberated from cyclic suffering, they were ready to hear about the cessation of suffering. However, Buddha was correct to make the truth of cessation the third truth and not the second. For, after having heard only the truth of suffering, even if one desires liberation and has the intention to attain the true cessation that is an elimination of suffering, one has not yet identified the actual cause of suffering and thus has not seen the possibility of overcoming this cause. One would not conceive the object required for liberation simultaneous with developing an intention actually to cease suffering.

Similarly, once there is an intention to manifest the cessation that is liberation, one wonders what path leads to this goal. Because such a thought is the entrance to the truth of the path, Buddha concluded the teaching on the four truths by explaining the truth of the path. Maitreya's *Sublime Continuum of the Mahayana* says:

> That to be known is the illness,
> That to be abandoned is its cause,
> That to be attained is happiness,
> That to be depended upon is the medicine.
> Just so are suffering and its cause,
> Its cessation and the path.

The teaching of the four noble truths appears many times in both the Hinayana and Mahayana scriptures. In this teaching, the One Gone Thus condensed the key essentials that explain how one is drawn into cyclic existence and how to leave it. Hence, this presentation is very important for the achievement of actual liberation. It is necessary to lead practitioners by stages to this most excellent practice. If one does not have true aversion for cyclic existence gained by means of contemplating the truth of suffering, the desire for liberation will be mere words and whatever one does will be a cause of suffering. If one does not fully identify the actions and afflictive emotions that are the root of cyclic existence by means of contemplating the truth of suffering's causes, it is like aiming an arrow without seeing the target. That is, one would miss the key realization of the path and would apprehend as the path to liberation that which is not the path. Thereafter one's efforts would be fruitless. Finally, if one does not understand that suffering and its causes must be abandoned, one cannot identify the liberation that eradicates them. Thus, though one might desire liberation, one is merely boasting.

8 The Conventional and Ultimate Minds of Enlightenment

The *Commentary on (Dzong-ka-ba's) "Foundation of All Excellence"* says:

> As long as we have desire and attachment, we will wander in cyclic existence. We should greatly fear this consequence. In order to stop cyclic existence we must enter the right path through desiring liberation. Finally, we reach the stages of the path for the highest practitioner, the Bodhisattva. We can attain liberation by following the three exceptional trainings, but we will liberate only ourselves from the suffering of cyclic existence, fulfilling only the minor purposes of ourselves and others. Therefore, Buddha taught that one must finally enter the Mahayana path.
>
> There exists in each living being the potential for attaining Buddhahood, called the Buddha-essence (*de bzhin gshegs pa'i snying po, tathāgatagarbha*), the "legacy abiding within", (*rang bzhin gnas rigs, prakṛtiṣṭhagotra*). This Buddha-essence is the emptiness of the mind, which is untainted by any defilement, existing as pure from the very beginning even though in the midst

123

of afflictive emotions. There is also the "developmental lineage" (rgyas 'gyur gyi rigs, paripuṣṭagotra), which is the cultivation of those mental states suitable for Buddhahood and is an attribute of the highest practitioners. Through this mental training one can produce the altruistic aspiration for highest enlightenment, the benefits of which are beyond measure. Then, it is very important to train in the Bodhisattva-deeds.

Thus, the mental training for the highest practitioner consists of first producing the altruistic aspiration for enlightenment and then learning the Bodhisattva-deeds. Dzong-ka-ba says in the Foundation of all Excellence:

> *Having seen that all beings, my former kind mothers,*
> *Have fallen like myself into the ocean of existence,*
> *May I practice the superior altruistic aspiration for enlightenment,*
> *Which assumes the obligation to free all beings.*
> (v.7)

I make obeisance at the lotus feet
Of Vajradhara, who is Shakyamuni, lord of the teaching,
Of Manjushri and Maitreya, teachers of
That which is profound and vast,
And of my lama, who embodies all objects of refuge.
With delight I will explain how to enter the supreme
vehicle.[51]

After undertaking many difficult religious practices, Shakyamuni Buddha attained perfect enlightenment and then remained in this world solely for the sake of guiding sentient beings who have been wandering in the limitless depths of ocean-like cyclic existence since beginningless time. Now that we have obtained a human life endowed with leisure and opportunity and have come in contact with the teaching, we should strive to follow the way of the

Teacher in order to fulfill the purpose of human life. To reach the high state of Buddhahood, it is necessary to travel the path that Buddha himself travelled, the Mahayana path of unified method and wisdom. The Hearers and Self-Enlightened Ones of the Hinayana turn away from worldly activities to attain merely their own liberation. However, it is only by entering the supreme path of unified method and wisdom that we enter Buddha's actual path. Unless we apply ourselves to this path, we will neither fulfill the aims of others nor accomplish our own highest aim.

Maudgalyayana and Shariputra, the Buddha's two chief disciples, were each intent on their own liberation. Although Maudgalyayana possessed supernormal powers and was able to fly, on one occasion his ability was impaired and he was beaten to death by a group of non-Buddhist ascetics. This occurred as a result of his misdeeds in a former lifetime. When Shariputra found Maudgalyayana dying and asked why he had not used his powers to escape, Maudgalyayana answered, "Not only was I unable to use my powers, I could not even remember Buddha's face."

The fact that Maudgalyayana had to undergo such suffering as an effect of his former misdeeds shows that, despite his special powers, he still fell short of the final goal, attainment of the perfect enlightenment of Buddhahood. Taking this example to heart, we should endeavor to attain perfect enlightenment through practice that unifies method and wisdom. Method is practice of the conventional mind of enlightenment (*kun rdzob byang chub kyi sems, saṃvṛti-bodhicitta*), and wisdom is practice of the ultimate mind of enlightenment (*don dam byang chub kyi sems, paramārtha-bodhicitta*). Through the former, we attain a Buddha's Form Body (*gzugs sku, rūpakāya*) and through the latter a Buddha's Truth Body (*chos sku, dharmakāya*). By relying on the conventional mind of enlightenment and the ultimate mind of enlightenment, like a snow goose relying on its wings, we can pass over the suffering of cyclic existence and reach perfect enlightenment.

The explanation of the practices for attaining Buddha-hood is divided into three parts: meditation on the conventional mind of enlightenment, meditation on the ultimate mind of enlightenment, and unification of these two objects of meditation.

Meditation on the Conventional Mind of Enlightenment

We cannot generate the altruistic aspiration to enlightenment (i.e., the conventional mind of enlightenment) of the Mahayana by merely desiring to attain Buddhahood for ourselves alone. If we desire to fulfill only our purpose, we will merely generate the altruistic aspiration to enlightenment of the Self-Enlightened Ones. Therefore, Maitreya said:

> To generate the altruistic aspiration to
>   enlightenment
> Means to desire perfect enlightenment for the sake
>   of others.

Just as water is needed to quench thirst, concern for others is crucial to the generation of the altruistic aspiration. And just as one must find a vessel to contain that water, so we need to attain Buddhahood to fulfill the aims of others.

To generate the altruistic aspiration to enlightenment, it is not sufficient to desire to help merely a limited number of beings; we must wish to help all beings without discrimination — from beings in hell to Bodhisattvas on the tenth stage. Because we ordinary persons discriminate among those who are friendly, unfriendly, or indifferent towards us, it is necessary from the outset to develop an attitude of equanimity towards all sentient beings.

This is achieved by recognizing that biases are based on delusion: Our partiality arises because we are unaware that we have wandered helplessly through limitless lifetimes in limitless cyclic existence and is further strengthened and maintained by our firm discrimination between friends and enemies of this life. One should remember that those who have been our friends in former lives may now be hostile towards us, while those who are not now hostile may have been very unkind to us previously. Even in this lifetime, our closest friends can become our enemies. Why then should we be so attached to some persons while abandoning others due to dislike? There is no justification for such discrimination. Attachment and hatred are the root of all non-virtue and suffering. We must recognize that because these two attitudes obstruct the development of enlightenment, they bar the door to our attainment of Buddhahood.

With equanimity as our basis, we can proceed to develop skill in meditation intent on the good of all beings. When we are accustomed to this kind of meditation, we can increase it limitlessly in all future rebirths until Buddhahood is attained. For this reason, we must begin to generate this altruistic aspiration right now.

First, consider that because cyclic existence is beginningless, you have been reborn a limitless number of times and thus there is no being who has not been your mother at least once. Constantly bear this thought in mind. For instance, regard the dog you hear barking at night as your old mother calling out to you. Thinking of each sentient being as your mother in past lives, reflect:

> When she was my mother and bore me in her womb, she guarded me as though I were a precious jewel. She cherished me even more than her own life. She happily provided me with every kind of benefit and protected me from all manner of harm. My mother of this lifetime has even provided me with a precious human birth endowed with leisure and opportunity. Her kindness is inconceivable.

Then consider how all sentient beings have been kind to you indirectly, acting as the basis of your well-being. For instance, that you now enjoy a human life endowed with leisure and opportunity is the effect of your practice of ethics in past existences. Ethics is, in essence, restraint from afflicting others; because sentient beings were the objects of your ethics, they are the indirect cause for your developing an attitude of non-harm.

Your present material enjoyments are the result of your former practice of giving (*sbyin pa, dāna*) and giving can exist only if others act as recipients of your gifts. Any physical beauty you may have is the result of your practice of patience, (*bzod pa, kṣānti*), and you could not learn patience without practicing it toward beings who do you harm.

To achieve the high state of Buddhahood, it is necessary to become skilled in all six perfections — giving, ethics, patience, effort, concentration, and wisdom — and each depends on sentient beings. Thus, insofar as both are essential to the achievement of Buddhahood, there is no difference in the kindness of Buddhas and of sentient beings.

Once you understand the kindness of all beings, it would be shameful not to repay their kindness. Think:

> Before Buddha attained perfect enlightenment, he was an ordinary being just as I am now and was similarly sustained by the kindness of innumerable sentient beings. Buddha repaid their kindness by undergoing many hardships for aeon after aeon until he attained Buddhahood. I, on the other hand, have neglected sentient beings and am therefore still immersed in this ocean of cyclic existence. Now, feeling deep shame, I will honestly try to repay their kindness by practicing the Bodhisattva-deeds.

However, it is not sufficient to repay sentient beings by providing them with mere defiled, worldly happiness. To give a trifle of defiled happiness is like giving salt water to a thirsty person. Not only does it fail to give final satisfaction, it arouses even stronger desire. Think:

> All beings, my old mothers, wished to free me from suffering and bring me happiness. Although they tried to the best of their abilities, they did not actually know the difference between help and

harm. Now that I can understand the causes of
affliction and the benefits of purification, I should
not mislead beings by appeasing them with worth-
less gifts as though they were mere children. I must
strive continually to repay their kindness in an
effective way.

To accomplish the purposes of others, you must have a
solid foundation of both equanimity, which eradicates flaws
in your desire to help others, and loving-kindness, which
motivates you to help others by regarding them as attrac-
tive. To accomplish the purposes of others means simply to
provide them with happiness and free them from suffering.
Like yourself, all beings are motivated even in dreams by a
desire for happiness and an aversion to suffering. Yet,
though they constantly seek happiness, they fail to find
genuine undefiled happiness, for their enjoyment inevitably
turns into suffering. Thus they remain fettered to the three
types of suffering by their afflictive emotions and previous
actions. Contemplating their sorrowful situation think:

How good it would be if all beings enjoyed undefiled happiness! May they attain such happiness! In
order that they may enjoy such happiness, I offer all
my happiness and virtue to them.

Because you have always placed the highest value on your
own aims, you have sought to provide only for your own
good and consequently have undergone all sorts of calami-
ties. Buddha, in contrast, forsook his own welfare, cherished
the welfare of others, and thereby perfected the highest
aims of both himself and others. This is the right choice.
Therefore you should think, "I will no longer be inflated by
egoism and will even give up my life in order to achieve
happiness for others." This is how to cultivate loving-
kindness. To cultivate compassion, think:

Just as the sick and injured cannot enjoy good food,
so all beings have been overpowered by constant

suffering for so many aeons that they cannot find
even a moment of real enjoyment. Their bodily,
verbal, and mental activities have been continually
driven along the course of nonvirtue by their afflictive emotions. As a result, their deeds plunge them
into the frightful abyss of the lower realms where
their suffering is so intense that they cannot bear it
even for an instant. In these realms, their suffering
continues unbroken for innumerable aeons, and
neither swooning nor death brings relief. Since all
those beings who have fallen into the hells are my
kind former mothers of previous lives, how can I be
happy? Let me take their mental and physical suffering upon myself in order that they may find
relief. How good it would be if they were free from
suffering! May they be free from all kinds of suffering! I will take the responsibility upon my own
shoulders to free them from suffering! Lamas and
gods, pray enable me to do this!

When you recite such prayers, visualize your lama before
you, appearing as Shakyamuni Buddha, with rays of light
emanating from his heart. Through the power of these rays,
all sentient beings' suffering and wrongdoing are separated
from them and brought into the limitless space before you.
When inhaling, imagine that your breath draws this suffering and wrongdoing into your body and that they eradicate
your selfish feeling. When exhaling, imagine that the light-
rays of the Buddhas, and Bodhisattvas' compassion draw out
your happiness and virtue and mix them equally with the
unending blessings of the Buddhas. Imagine that you thus
establish all beings whose number is limitless as space in
complete happiness. In this way, meditate on alternating
"giving and taking", giving your happiness to others and
taking their suffering upon yourself.

After meditating for a long time on compassion and loving kindness, close the meditation by visualizing that the
task of promoting the welfare of all beings falls upon your

shoulders. Think:

> It is now imperative for me to attain Buddhahood as
> there is no one but myself to free these beings from
> suffering and bring them undefiled happiness. I
> must strive to attain Buddhahood.

Thus the altruistic aspiration to attain Buddhahood requires, as its indispensable support, the firm intention to
help others. Some people, however, attempt to generate
this aspiration by meditating solely on their own intention
to attain Buddhahood, without grounding their meditation
in the intention to help others. This is not a skillful method
for generating the altruistic aspiration to enlightenment.

Certainly, it is correct to meditate on the qualities of the
Buddha's body, speech, and mind, but at the same time we
should recognize that such qualities as Samantabhadra Buddha's body of radiant light are necessary principally for the
purpose of quickly fulfilling others' aims and thus presup-
pose the intention to help others. While we should make the
desire to acquire such qualities an integral part of our
practice, we should not do so with the primary aim of
obtaining such a body for our own use.

Just as a wish-fulfilling jewel has an unlimited ability to
procure material wealth, the mere generation of the altruistic aspiration to enlightenment has an unlimited ability to
purify us of our former non-virtuous actions and increase
our store of merit. The ability of the altruistic aspiration to
surpass the virtues of Hearers and Self-Enlightened Ones is
found in its four limitless aspects:

1 limitless number of sentient beings
2 limitless good qualities of enlightenment
3 limitless time
4 limitless deeds.

The altruistic aspiration to highest enlightenment has
two aspects: the aspirational mind of enlightenment (*smon
sems*) and the practical mind of enlightenment (*'jug sems*).

Both have the same altruistic desire to attain highest enlightenment, but the former is like wishing to go to a place whereas the latter is like actually going there. The aspirational mind has the first two limitless aspects: its object is to help a limitless number of sentient beings and to attain the limitless good qualities of highest enlightenment.

After generating the aspirational mind, one takes the Bodhisattva vow and generates the practical mind of enlightenment. In addition to the first two limitless aspects, the practical mind has the final two limitless aspects: one accumulates merit for a limitless amount of time because of the influence of the Bodhisattva vow's promises, and one engages in the limitless deeds of a Bodhisattva. Because the practical mind has all four limitless aspects, its benefit greatly exceeds that of the aspirational mind. Thus, it is said that there is no method for intensifying the aspirational mind superior to keeping the practical mind as our objective. The practical mind of enlightenment increases our accumulation of merit ceaselessly because of the constant power of the promises of the Bodhisattva vow. From the moment of possessing the practical mind of enlightenment, we are as if setting out on the highway to our destination — we commence the three immeasurable aeons of cultivating virtue that are required to reach Buddhahood.

Meditation on the Ultimate Mind of Enlightenment
The ultimate mind of enlightenment results from realization of emptiness. We must understand it as the indispensable seed for attaining Buddhahood and reflect on the necessity for our own capacity to attain that highest enlightenment.

First, consider the following. We cannot deliver others without first delivering ourselves, and in order to deliver ourselves it is absolutely necessary to eradicate the root of cyclic existence.

All schools of Buddhism attempt to define the root of cyclic existence, but their interpretations differ according to the depth of their understanding. In their commentaries on the Perfection of Wisdom Sutras (*shes rab kyi pha rol tu phyin pa'i mdo, prajñāpāramitāsūtra*), Nagarjuna and his disciples described Buddha's thought in expounding those sutras. Understanding these commentaries is the only door to liberation; there is no alternative.

According to these texts, the root of all cyclic existence is the erroneous conception of inherent existence (*rang bzhin, svabhāva*). To eradicate this root, it is necessary to develop the wisdom that realizes selflessness, the lack of inherent existence. Once this wisdom is attained, we will never go wrong again. Just as a common candle surpasses even a lump of a gold in luminosity, so even a portion of this wisdom surpasses all other virtues in its ability to dispel the darkness of egoism. It is common to all three vehicles — the vehicles of Hearers, Self-Enlightened Ones, and Bodhisattvas. However, an extensive and complete investigation of this wisdom is taught especially in the Mahayana. Such investigation purifies us from even the most subtle defilement of habitual tendencies, just as a good cleanser removes the most subtle stains. This kind of defilement, the potencies left by former actions, is the most difficult to remove and disappears only with the attainment of Buddhahood. Thus, it is imperative that we meditate on the wisdom that realizes selflessness as it is discussed in the Mahayana.

Our Capacity to Attain Buddhahood

That we have the capacity to attain Buddhahood can be understood by investigating the second section of the Perfection of Wisdom literature, which explains the practice of the path. There it is stated that the altruistic aspiration to enlightenment is absolutely necessary for the attainment of Buddhahood. Once we generate this aspiration, it functions in unison with other causes within our mental continuum, and the attainment of Buddhahood will certainly result.

Although the scriptures speak explicitly of three vehicles,

the doctrine of a triple vehicle is Buddha's expedient for guiding his three types of disciples — Hearers, Self-Enlightened Ones, and Bodhisattvas. Ultimately, there is only one vehicle for reaching the final goal of Buddhahood, the Bodhisattva Vehicle, or Mahayana. In his *Precise Commentary*, Dharmakirti establishes the existence of one final vehicle by citing the reason of impermanence. With this reason, Dharmakirti shows that the mind is not inherently defiled and can therefore be corrected. Thus, ultimately, the proof for the existence of a single final vehicle is the mind's lack of inherent existence. Buddha indicated this by using the term "naturally liberated" (*rang bzhin gyis yongs su mya ngan las 'das pa*). By this Buddha did not mean that the mind is exclusively pure, but that its afflictive emotions are only temporary. Just as the tarnish on gold disappears when the gold is polished, so the afflictive emotions will disappear when the mind is purified through practice. Because the afflictive emotions are only adventitious, all beings have the capacity to attain Buddhahood.

Once we are convinced of the necessity for the ultimate mind of enlightenment and of our capacity to attain Buddhahood, we will delight in generating the conventional mind of enlightenment and strive with vigor to meditate on the ultimate mind of enlightenment.

How to Unify the Conventional and Ultimate Minds of Enlightenment

In order to practice the Mahayana, we must unify wisdom, the practice of the ultimate mind of enlightenment, with method, the practice of the conventional mind of enlightenment. Method and wisdom are the causes of obtaining the two bodies of a Buddha. Method, as the accumulation of merit, is the cause of obtaining the Form Body. Wisdom, as the accumulation of knowledge, is the cause of obtaining the Truth Body. The practice of both method and wisdom protects us from falling into either of the two extremes: solitary peace and cyclic existence. Method eradicates the extreme of remaining in the solitary peace of nirvana; wisdom eradicates the extreme of remaining in cyclic existence. Method alone cannot free us from afflictive emotions. This is what Maitreya meant when he wrote that the merits of giving, ethics, patience, effort, and concentration are truly effective only when conjoined with wisdom.

We should be diligent in practicing the six perfections, aware of their benefits and the obstacles to their practice. After taking up this practice, purification and liberation will arise. When compassion is merged with wisdom, there will be no fetters of laziness and attachment; what is accomplished will be pure and practical. Just as a lamp and its rays of light are inseparable, so too are wisdom and method. By conjoining these two we can produce the manifold realization of the Vajrayana path. We can then attain without delay the high state of Vajradhara Buddha.

9 A Magician's Illusions

The *Commentary on (Ḍzong-ka-ḅa's) "Foundation of All Excellence"* cites the *King of Meditative Stabilizations Sutra* (*ting nge 'dzin gyi rgyal po, samādhirāja*):

> *Illusory, like a city of celestial musicians,*
> *Like a mirage, like a dream —*
> *Meditate that designations are empty in nature;*
> *Understand all existence in this way.*

THE EXAMPLE OF A MAGICIAN'S ILLUSION[52]

The attainment of liberation and Buddhahood, whether through the path of the sutras or of secret mantra (tantra), requires thoroughly overcoming one's perception of things as inherently existent along with all adherence to this perception. Because it is so difficult to understand *how* ordinary perceptions and related conceptions are mistaken, it is often explained using the example of a magician's illusion.

A magician can create the illusion of a horse by casting a spell over a small stone, causing it to appear as a horse. When the magician manifests a stone as a horse, he sees the stone as a horse but does not adhere to it as a real horse.

Deluded spectators both see it as a horse and adhere to it as one. People who arrive after the spell has been cast are not under its power; they neither see the stone as a horse nor adhere to it as such.

In this example, the magician exemplifies an ordinary person who realizes the general significance of emptiness. Although phenomena are seen as if truly, or inherently, existent, they are not adhered to as such. The spectators exemplify ordinary persons who have not understood emptiness and who therefore see phenomena as truly existent and adhere to them as such. The people who arrive afterwards exemplify Superiors (*'phags pa, ārya*) who have realized emptiness directly. They neither see phenomena as truly existent nor do they adhere to them as such.

Although the stone appears as a horse to the magician and the deluded spectators, how it appears to them will differ. The magician, although perceiving the stone as a horse, understands that it appears as a horse through the influence of the mind. He does not take the appearance of the horse to be the product of natural causes and conditions operating independently of the cognizing mind. The deluded spectators, however, take the appearance of the horse as a sign that a real horse is present and understand the appearance to arise through the existence of a real horse.

If, as this example indicates, things do not exist precisely in accordance with how they appear, what type of existence do they have? In general there are three modes of existence:

1 the existence established in a phenomenon by its natural causes and conditions (*gnyug ma'i rgyu rkyen*) or substantial cause (*nyer len gyi rgyu*), like the heat of fire caused by the fire

2 the existence that originates in a phenomenon through external conditions (*phyi'i rkyen*) or cooperative causes (*lhan cig byed rkyen*), like heat that is produced in a lump of iron by exposure to fire

3 the mode of existence that is attributed to a phenomenon by the mind (*blos bcos pa*) like the heat experienced as

inhering in a lump of iron that has been made to appear red-hot by the power of sorcery.

An illusory appearance possesses this third mode of existence, that created by the mind. How is this? At the time of working his sorcery, a sorcerer internally reflects, "That burning red lump of iron will not burn anything." At the time of creating an illusion, a magician internally reflects "That stone looks exactly like a horse, but is not a horse." Neither the sorcerer nor the magician are deceived by the appearance of their respectively created objects. Both understand through valid cognition the mode of existence possessed by the horse and the sensation of heat (as explained below).

Another example of erroneous perception occurs when a rope coiled in a dark place is mistaken for a snake. The appearance of the rope as a snake and the appearance of the stone as a horse are alike in being mistaken perceptions. However, the horse is identified by valid cognition but the rope-snake is not, and thus the error involved differs in the two cases. This is explained in Dzong-ka-ba's *Illumination of the Thought* (*dbu ma dgongs pa rab gsal*) and Kay-drup's *Thousand Topics* (*stong thun*), two works explaining Middle Way School (*dbu ma pa, mādhyamika*) philosophy. Dzong-ka-ba and his disciples do not detail how the appearance of a snake is or is not produced from a rope, but instead devote their efforts to proving that when the stone appears as a horse, *something* appears from the stone. They illustrate the three modes of existence described previously as follows. When a brown rope coiled in a dark hollow appears like a snake, this appearance possesses a mode of existence that is produced by an external cause, the darkness. When a small stone that is unaffected by a magician's spells or other transformative substances is seen, it cannot be perceived as a horse, and its mode of existence is produced by its own natural causes and conditions. When a small stone affected by spells is seen as a horse, its mode of existence is created by the mind.

In short, the rope is identified as a snake by an erroneous consciousness, and the stone is identified as an illusory horse by an essentially valid cognition. Thus, we should understand generally that when a magician manifests an illusion, the stone becomes the entity of an illusory horse.

This can be further understood by investigating relevant assertions from the various schools of Buddhism. The Buddhist tenets developed in India are divided into four main schools — the Hinayana tenets of the Great Exposition School (*bye brag smra ba, vaibhāṣika*) and Sūtra School (*mdo sde pa, sautrāntika*), and the Mahayana tenets of the Mind Only School (*sems tsam pa, cittamātra*) and Middle Way School (*dbu ma pa, mādhyamika*); the latter are further divided into the Autonomy School (*rang rgyud pa, svātantrika*) and Consequence School (*thal 'gyur pa, prāsaṅgika*). The Middle Way Autonomy School in turn contains the subcategories of Sutra Autonomy Middle Way School (*mdo sde spyod pa'i dbu ma rang rgyud pa, sautrāntika-svātantrika-mādhyamika*) and Yogic Autonomy Middle Way School (*rnal 'byor spyod pa'i dbu ma rang rgyud pa, yogācāra-svātantrika-mādhyamika*).

Both Autonomy Middle Way Schools assert that a phenomenon possesses a mode of existence that is posited solely by the power of its appearing to a correct mind.[53] Both agree that the word "solely" in the phrase above does not repudiate an object's establishment from its own side (*rang ngos nas grub pa, svarūpasiddhi*). Further, when the Sutra Autonomy Middle Way School asserts a phenomenon to be posited solely by the power of appearing to a correct mind, they do not use the word "solely" to repudiate external existence. For, the Sutra Autonomy Middle Way School asserts external existence whereas the Yogic Autonomy Middle Way School does not.

Both Autonomists say that when we see a magician's illusion, we see, for example, a small stone as a horse. Since it possesses a mode of existence posited by the mind, the illusory horse exists. The appearance occurs only when the stone is affected by the magician's spells or transformative substances. Therefore, according to the Autonomists, the horse is established from the side of its basis of magical transformation, that is, the small stone. This is why Autonomists assert establishment from its own side or establishment from the side of the basis of designation (*gdags gzhi*).

The Sutra Autonomy Middle Way School differs significantly from the Sutra School. Proponents of the Sutra School say that self-character (*rang mtshan*, *svalakṣaṇa*) is posited by the power of appearing to direct cognition; Proponents of the Sutra Autonomy Middle Way School say that self-character is posited by the power of appearing to a correct mind. The two systems differ because the Sutra School maintains that the existence possessed by the self-character that appears to direct cognition is a final (*mthar thug*) mode of existence and that therefore self-character ultimately exists (*don dam par yod pa*). The Autonomists, in contrast, consider that although all phenomena do appear to a correct mind, their way of appearing does not possess a final mode of existence because a final mode of existence does not ultimately exist.

How Illusions are Posited
A person's mind possesses many kinds of mental factors. In the Autonomy Middle Way School, all phenomena are posited as existing by the power of their appearance to a *correct* mind. If they were posited as existing solely by the power of their appearance to any kind of mind, we would have to say that a rope is in fact a snake. Thus, it is essential to use the word "correct" to specify that the mind perceiving such an illusion is not defiled by any superficial cause of error.

The illusory horse exists, that is, it exists by way of its ability to appear before a correct mind. When the magician manifests a small stone as a horse, he first has to apply some spells, ointments, or other transformative substances to the small stone. Yet, as long as neither he nor any deluded spectator looks at the stone, there is no illusory horse. The illusory horse can be said to come into existence only when the magician or deluded spectator observes the stone. At that time, an illusory horse is posited by both of them, but the magician establishes it by valid cognition whereas the deluded spectator does not.

However, all aspects of the magician's perception are not valid. Like the deluded spectator, his visual consciousness that perceives the stone's appearance as a horse cannot validly cognize an illusory horse because it is not a correct mind. As Dzong-ka-ba says in his *Illumination of the Thought*, both the deluded spectator's and the magician's eye consciousnesses are incorrect due to being affected by a cause of error, namely the magical ointment, spells, and so on.

What kind of valid cognition takes the illusory horse as its object? It does not exist in the mind of the deluded spectator, for no valid cognition arises in this person to perceive the illusory horse as illusory. Therefore, there can be no valid cognition other than by the visual consciousness of the magician. However, the magician's visual consciousness, which sees the stone as a horse, is not valid because it is an erroneous consciousness that is mistaken as to the object that appears to it (*snang yul, pratibhāsaviṣaya*). In what sense, then, does the magician have valid cognition? The magician's visual consciousness acts as an immediately preceding condition (*de ma thag rkyen, samanantarapratyaya*) for a thought which posits the horse as mere illusion. Then, although the magician continues to see the horse, he knows that the horse is merely appearing to a mistaken visual consciousness since he has determined that the apparent horse is not real.

In short, according to Dzong-ka-ba's *Great Exposition of the Stages of the Path*, when the illusory horse appears, the magician sees it with his visual consciousness and knows without doubt that it is not an actual horse. The illusory horse is identified by thought, and thus exists as imputed by thought. Thought, however, only establishes that the illusory horse is not a real horse; it does not establish that the illusory horse exists. What kind of mind establishes that the illusory horse exists? Dzong-ka-ba says in his *Illumination of the Thought* that the Proponents of the Yogic Autonomy Middle Way School — Shantarakshita and his followers — assert that self-cognition (*rang rig, svasaṃvedana*), which only takes a mental object, establishes that the illusory horse exists. He also says that the Proponents of the Sutra Autonomy Middle Way School — Bhavaviveka and his followers — assert that direct sensory cognition establishes that the illusory horse exists.

Does the illusory horse exist or not? I leave this question to be considered by scholars.

An Illustration of the Example of a Magician's Illusion
Dzong-ka-ba says in his *Praise of Dependent-Arising (rten 'brel bstod pa)*:[54]

> Therefore all things which come forth dependently
> Are from the first completely free of self-nature.
> Yet they appear to have self-nature
> And thus are said to be like a magician's illusion.
>   (v.27)

I will comment briefly on this verse. When a magician creates the illusion of a horse, bull, or anything else, this will appear to the eye through the power of the magician's spell or transformative substances. These objects appear to a mistaken eye consciousness. This is a suitable example for illustrating their lack of self-nature; yet, when we want to know the deep significance of this example, we must understand that those objects appear solely through the influence of a mistaken mental consciousness. How is this so? The following example of illusion was requested from Geshe Drom by his teacher Atisha, and was written down in the scriptures of the Ga-dam-ba lineage.

A magician named Dawa Sangbo, who lived in the city of Shravasti, had a friend named Bel. One day the magician suggested that his friend should study magic.

"Some day you might find it very useful," he said.

"Of what use could this be in the future? I would rather have a horse right now," Bel replied.

Dawa Sangbo thought, "He is very stupid. I can easily fool him."

The following morning after breakfast, while his wife was washing the breakfast dishes, Bel started his day's work by stretching yarn across the porch. Dawa Sangbo came up to the house riding a beautiful horse. He asked, "Do you want to buy this horse?"

"How can I buy a horse when I have no money?" Bel replied.

"That's all right. I'll take your yarn in exchange for the horse."

Bel then thought, "A horse for the yarn? I will trick him." So he said, "That sounds like a good price. I will buy your horse."

"Then you had better come out and see how it rides," replied the magician.

As soon as Bel mounted the horse, it flew off at breakneck speed. He travelled all day until sunset when the horse finally stopped in a deserted valley.

Bel thought, "This wicked horse has deceived me."

He looked around and saw a cottage with smoke rising from its chimney. When he knocked at the cottage door, an old woman came out.

He thought, "Oh good, someone is here. If human, all is well. If not ... Whether or not, I am completely bewildered tonight and have no choice; where else can I go? In the woods I might be eaten by tigers and wolves. I had better stay here." He inquired, "Is this an inn where I could get some shelter for the night?"

The woman cordially invited him in and introduced him to her three daughters. They gave him delicious food and drink and he related to them the strange events of the day. Then they informed him that he was on a deserted island

and there was no way to go out.

The old lady said, "My husband has died, and this house and land need a master. Please marry one of my daughters."

Since Bel was stranded on the island and had no idea where he was, he decided to stay and accept the old lady's offer. His past life and former wife soon faded from his memory, and he devoted all his love and energy to his new wife and the three children she bore him. One summer evening the family went out for a walk. The wife strolled through the woods while Bel took the children down to the river to play. The moon rose in the clear evening sky and one of the children, intrigued by the moon's image in the river, jumped in to catch it. While Bel was trying to rescue him from the swift current, another child, thinking it was all a game, jumped in after the first. Bel was in two minds as to what to do.

He thought, "By helping one, I will lose the other."

He lost them both and then saw his third child being carried off by a tiger. All his shouting for help was in vain. Grief-stricken, he lost consciousness. When his wife found him she revived him and asked what had happened. Told about the tragic death of her children, she was overcome by grief, and hurled herself into the river where she too drowned.

Bel, tearing out his hair in grief, lamented, "Now all is lost! I have no merit whatsoever, I was separated from my former family when they were alive and from my new family by death. It is better to die here, too!"

Then he noticed that the handful of hair he had torn out was white. Wondering how he had grown so old, still deeply immersed in sorrow, he wandered away from the scene of the tragedy and soon found himself in another country. Suddenly he realized that he was in front of his own former house. He looked around and found his wife inside, singing a sweet song while washing the breakfast dishes.

Indignant that she did not take special notice of him, he

angrily chided, "What have you done today? Haven't you even finished the wash?" He had completely lost trust in her and reproached her, saying, "Here you are singing sweet songs, disregarding my trouble. I was lost for so many years and you didn't even miss me, let alone search for me. You act as though there were nothing to worry about. Now that I am back, aren't you happy?"

His wife, trying to understand his anger thought, "Someone must have cast a spell upon him." She then said, "Husband, what has happened to you?"

He replied, 'Wife, I have been separated from you for years. You can't even imagine what has happened to me."

"Husband, what are you talking about? You do not understand. You have been deluded by your friend the magician. Look here." And she showed him his unbroken yarn.

Bel now began to doubt: "Well, perhaps my wife is right and I am completely wrong, but is it possible to be mistaken about so many years and about my children's death one after the other?" Still not quite free from the illusion, he tried to figure out the length of time. He thought, "There are twelve months in a year; thirty days in a month; twenty-four hours in a day and night. How could I have wandered so far in so short a time? Somehow my wife is deceiving me."

Again he went to the porch and saw his unbroken yarn. That sight broke the spell and destroyed his doubts.

After some days Bel's magician friend, Dawa Sangbo, passed by. "Well" the magician said, "I haven't seen you for a long time. Where have you been all these years?"

Bel related all of his experiences to him.

"Phu!" said the magician. "All that is illusion. Nothing is real. You never saw your wife and three children. How could your bodily experiences have taken place? How could you go so far without stepping out of your house for a moment? How could you experience so many years of suffering? The suffering of cyclic existence is just like that.

Although we wander for aeons, it is just like your journey.

Old age is like your white hair,
Youth like the death of your children.
Enemies are like that treacherous river,
Relatives like the old woman, mother, and children.
Homeland is like that land,
Sunrise and sunset like your arrival.
Holding as real that which is not
Is like your recent experience.

Householder Bel, don't give up investigating:
All is empty of self-nature from the beginning.
Understand this through hearing the song of your wife,
Through seeing your unbroken thread,
And through practicing deep meditation right now.
Understand that all subjects and objects,
Like the city Shravasti and so on,
Are similar to your recent experience.

Examine this again and again,
Then you will understand.
By the power of meditation, you will see its meaning.
Although you formerly did not believe your wife,
When you searched
Did you find a real self-nature?
Although you wandered so far,
Not until now do you understand."

Bel realized that he had been deceived by the magician's spell. He understood everything to be like a magician's illusion and resolved to investigate its significance repeatedly.

Later, when Bel was an old man, Dawa Sangbo again showed him the horse and asked him to buy it. Bel neither saw the horse nor did he hear the offer to sell it. He realized that everything appears merely through the influence of a mistaken mind. Likewise, we must realize that all appearances — inanimate objects and our own and others' activities of body, speech, and mind — are like an illusion from first to last.

Dzong-ka-b̄a's *Foundation of All Excellence* says:

> By quieting attraction to wrong objects
> And properly analyzing the meaning of reality
> Bless me to quickly produce in myself
> The path of unified tranquillity (meditation) and
>   insight (wisdom). (v.9)

10 The Foundation of All Excellence

At the beginning of his spiritual career, the great being who was to become known as Shakyamuni Buddha first generated the altruistic aspiration to highest enlightenment in both its aspirational and practical forms.[55] Then for three incalculable great aeons he accumulated the collections of merit and wisdom, which consist of the six perfections. He then attained the perfection of life, Buddhahood, for the sake of all living beings.

He next imparted to his disciples the precious nectar of the holy teaching with all its eighty-four thousand aggregates. By this act he set all beings on the right path, maturing those who were not yet mature, liberating those who were mature, and bringing to perfection those who were liberated.

All Buddha's essential teachings are included in the "lam rim" teachings — teachings on the stages of the path to enlightenment. There are many benefits in hearing and studying this teaching; to name just a few, one will understand the entire teaching, turn away from wrongdoing, give up senseless activities, and attain nirvana. This book is a condensed presentation that contains all the meanings of the key instructions for the stages of the path to enlightenment.

The very root of this path is the practice of reliance on a spiritual teacher. Buddha stated in sutra that to rely properly on the spiritual teacher, one must conceive of oneself as a sick person, of the spiritual teacher as a doctor, of his precepts as medicine, and of earnest practice as the cure. To increase one's faith in the spiritual teacher, Buddha said that one must rely on him with a mind that is like earth, never tired of its burden; with a mind immutable as a diamond, never changing in its resolve; and with a mind like a devoted attendant, doing all tasks without having to be told.

For those fortunate persons who rely properly on a spiritual teacher, it is very important to enter the mental practice of contemplating how difficult this human life of leisure and opportunity is to find. This is the first practice for beginning practitioners of Buddha's teaching and produces the motivation to accomplish the holy teaching.

For a beginningless stream of lifetimes we have wandered in leisureless conditions, such as in the three states of unfortunate beings, because of the influence of our actions and afflictive emotions. Now, this one time, we have obtained a human life endowed with both leisure and opportunity. This good fortune is the convergence of a great deal of virtuous karma, such as meeting with a holy spiritual teacher. Because this life is free from the eight conditions for being without leisure, we have the time to practice the teaching. Once we have the ten conditions for opportunity, we have all the inner and outer causes for realizing the teaching.

When we consider the precepts concerning this human life — the obstacles to obtaining it, its actual nature, its causes and effects, and the examples concerning it — we see how very rare it is. This life is more precious than a universe filled with wish-fulfilling jewels, for it enables us to accomplish the ten virtuous deeds that cause future birth as humans or gods and, beyond that, can even cause attainment of the adamantine body. With this life we can also generate the altruistic aspiration for enlightenment, achieve the six perfections, and fulfill the three trainings [ethics, meditative stabilization, and wisdom], which lead to omniscience and the assured good of liberation.

Understanding the importance of this, do not ruin yourself senselessly with inner and outer distractions, such as sleep and laziness, or by heedless involvement in the eight worldly concerns. Always be conscientious. Hearing, thinking, and meditating on Buddha's doctrine by day and by night, generate a mind that desires to take up the essence of the holy teaching in both its aspects of verbal exposition and experiential insight. Once you have applied such thoughts to practice, strive to use the methods learned to make meaningful this human life with its leisure and opportunity.

Having produced a desire to utilize the essence, that is, to take full advantage, of our life, we must learn how to do so, stage by stage. In this we begin with the realization of impermanence and the truth of suffering, and continue through the great practice of the highest Bodhisattva's deeds. After we have ascertained through hearing and thinking the levels, enumerations, and nature of the path, we must meditate on them without confusing their stages. This is the great key of practice.

There is no security in obtaining this life of leisure and opportunity, for conditions do not allow us to stay as we are and in each moment the life flow fluctuates, moving toward death. We perish as quickly as the bubbles in a puddle of rain water. Again and again we must contemplate this impermanence, remembering that we have no power to remain forever and no certainty as to when we will die. Without being attached to the worldly enjoyments of this life, which are like chaff in the wind and of no future benefit, we must turn our minds away from the concerns of this life and decide to practice immediately the holy teaching, the method for attaining lasting happiness.

We can understand the impermanence of our human life

through contemplating how the days, months, and years steadily pass by as we approach nearer and nearer to our death. Although we do not wish to die, we have no ability to live on. Birth, sickness, old age, and death advance one by one as methodically as the turning of a mill wheel. That demon, the lord of death, awaits us like a hungry shark. There are an inconceivable number of conditions that bring about death, but none that can extend our life. For instance, though we eat food in order to sustain our bodies, we could suddenly choke and die.

In this world, everyone, whether great or small, rich or poor, will be overpowered by the lord of death. Those whom we have seen die were always hopeful not to go, collecting wealth and raising children, etc. Yet they died accompanied only by their virtuous and non-virtuous actions. Do you not see this when you consider your own condition? Do you not see and hear about the deaths of your spiritual teachers, loved ones, enemies, those your own age, those younger and older? All living beings in this world must die, and the longest they can live is about one hundred years. Thus we are born to die.

Furthermore, we do not know whether we will die today or tomorrow. Even those who have some idea of their life's duration do not fear death. They do not give gifts or make any other preparation, but die while conducting themselves as they usually do.

At the time of death our spiritual teachers, parents, children, siblings, relatives, attendants, and all our wealth cannot come with us. No one can share our suffering at that time; we must die alone just as we are born alone. We may now have close friends, houses, land, and valuable treasures, and not wish to separate from them for even a moment. However, we will have to leave them and travel death's terrifying path all alone. Though we may have accumulated wealth through wrongdoing, we alone will suffer the consequences of those misdeeds. All that wealth is only taken by our children and relatives — what use is it to us at the time of death? Even our dear body must be given up completely at that time. As you have wandered all alone without independence and are born by the power of your actions, do not commit more wrongs for the sake of your livelihood.

Regarding what may happen after death, Buddha once taught King Bimbisara, "My friend, there is nothing other than virtue and sin. Virtue is the cause of rebirth as a human or divine being and of liberation. Sin is the cause of rebirth as an unfortunate being and of suffering." Thus it is taught in sutra that we do not simply disappear after death but must take rebirth into either a happy or unhappy condition.

Just as a shadow follows the body, our virtuous and non-virtuous actions follow us into our next life. The three gradations of the ten virtuous deeds — small, medium, and great — lead respectively to rebirth as a human, as a god of the desire realm, or as a god of the higher realms. They have the conditioning effects of giving rise to a long life and good health and the positioning effect that one will abide in a place of great beauty. In short, these virtues result in happiness which increases until perfect omniscience is obtained.

The three gradations of the ten non-virtuous deeds — small, medium, and great — lead respectively to rebirth as an animal, a hungry ghost, or a being in hell. They have the conditioning effect that even when you rise out of these unfortunate births and are reborn as a human being, you will have a short life with much illness and will enjoy killing others. The positioning effect of such actions is that wherever you live will be disagreeable. In short, we face only wretched results from non-virtuous actions.

Thus, we are certain to meet the effects of deeds done and will never meet effects from those we did not do. What we have done will not decay, and the effects will in fact multiply. Buddha taught in the *Sutra on the Many Kinds of Actions* (*mdo sde las brgya ba*):

The actions of embodied beings
Will never be lost in even one hundred aeons —
They will simply give their effects
When their conditions and time arise.

We must find strong conviction in these true words of the Compassionate Teacher.

If one assembled in palpable form all one's non-virtuous actions accumulated from beginningless time, the mass would be greater than the highest mountain or vastest ocean. If in this life we heedlessly heap up more wrong actions, we will surely be reborn in the lower states of unfortunate beings: the hot and cold hells, the hungry ghost realm, and the animal realm. There we will experience intense suffering that lasts for hundreds of thousands of human years. Contemplating this, we must abandon all wrongdoing such as the ten non-virtuous deeds. The best course of action is not to produce even the intention to do the slightest wrong, let alone actually to engage in grave wrongdoing. The middling course is to abandon a non-virtuous deed after having begun it. The least we can do if we commit a wrong is to repent and confess it, restraining ourselves by promising never to do it again and then generating the altruistic aspiration to enlightenment.

We must, with mindfulness and introspection, remain heedful day and night to attain all the great masses of virtue, such as the ten virtuous deeds, which are the abandonment of the ten non-virtuous deeds. Best is to accomplish whatever we can. Middling is not to give them up, even if we cannot do them right now. At the least, we should fervently pray and aspire actually to do them at some future time.

To describe karma in more detail, let us discuss the ten non-virtuous and ten virtuous actions, or deeds. The ten non-virtues are killing, stealing, sexual misconduct, lying, slander, harsh speech, senseless speech, covetousness, harmful mind, and wrong view. These ten are obstacles to a fortunate rebirth, liberation, and omniscience, and certainly lead to rebirth in the three states of unfortunate beings. There we will suffer for many, many lifetimes and finally, by our former virtuous actions, so difficult to attain, will be reborn as a human being.

Yet even in this newly obtained human life we will suffer the continuing effect of the non-virtuous actions that led us to the unfortunate rebirths. Due to having killed living beings, we will suffer much illness and have a short human life. Because we took that which was not given, we will have few resources and these will be under others' control. From the non-virtuous actions of sexual misconduct, anyone we hire will be recalcitrant and our spouse will be quarrelsome. Because of lying, our words will not be respected and we will be deceived by others. Through our former acts of slander, those whom we hire or are associated with will always be wicked and contrary. Having spoken harshly, in our human life we will hear only unpleasant and contentious words. Because of our former senseless speech, we will always hear false and unreliable words from others. If we were previously reborn as an unfortunate being because of covetousness, we will when we are once again reborn as a human be constantly dissatisfied and desirous. Because of formerly having had a harmful mind, we will be involved in harmful and unbeneficial actions and will receive such actions from others as well. By our former wrong views, we will again fall into wrong and deceitful views.

The ten virtuous deeds are to abandon the ten non-virtues. They lead to rebirth in the fortunate states in general and, in addition, each gives rise to specific effects — such as a long life through abandoning killing, great resources through abandoning stealing, an agreeable spouse through forsaking sexual misconduct, no disrespect from others by giving up lying, and faithful and truthful associates from forsaking slander. In short, abandoning the ten non-virtues is the cause of liberation.

When we consider the cultivation of virtue more specifically, it is very important to obtain a human life endowed with the eight maturing qualities, for such a life is highly efficacious for attaining Buddhahood. These eight are: a long life, pleasing appearance, high birth, wealth, pure speech, influence and renown, male form, and physical and mental strength. With such a human life we can cultivate many virtues for a long time. We will attract disciples, and they will follow our instructions. Each quality has its specific cause. For instance, by abandoning pride we will receive high birth, abandoning anger brings a pleasing appearance, forsaking jealousy leads to a radiant appearance, and abandoning stinginess gives rise to wealth.

Having contemplated the importance of this human life with its leisure and opportunity, the imminence of death, and the law of the effects of actions, we must enter the practice of rejecting wrong actions and cultivating virtue. Buddha said in the *Great Nirvana Sutra* (*yongs su mya ngan las 'das pa chen po'i mdo, mahāparinirvāṇasūtra*):

> Those who always want happiness
> For themselves and others do no wrong.
> When the childlike who desire happiness
> Do wrong, they must suffer the results.

Thus once we have deepened our faith in the teaching, we must day and night carefully examine our physical, verbal, and mental actions, turning away from wrongdoing and cultivating virtue. Should we in spite of great effort to do this still do wrong, we should make confession, utilizing the four powers. In the same way we should correct also the transgressions of any vows we have taken. This concludes the stages of the path for beings of small capacity.

Next we progress to the stages of the path set forth for beings of middling capacity. By making effort, beginning with mindfulness of death and continuing through the cultivation of right actions and the rejection of wrong, we will attain rebirth as a fortunate being. Yet, at this stage, we are still tightly bound by actions and afflictive emotions and in the future will certainly fall back into the lower states of unfortunate beings. Bound in the prison of the three realms of cyclic existence, we will continue to be tortured on the rack of the three kinds of suffering. Therefore, we must produce a desire for release and then travel the path to liberation. Concerning the former, Dzong-ka-ḃa says in the *Foundation of All Excellence*:

> The door to all misery is our dissatisfaction with
>   enjoyments.
> Having realized the ills of worldly marvels,
> Which offer us no security,
> May I be strongly intent on the bliss of liberation.
>   (v.5)

The desire for liberation is absolutely essential for entering either the Hinayana or Mahayana path. To generate this desire, it is necessary to consider the ills of cyclic existence in accordance with the first two noble truths — the truth of suffering and the truth of suffering's cause — and in accordance with the teaching of the twelve-linked chain of dependent-arising.

To understand the truth of suffering, we must consider the suffering of each of the six types of beings in cyclic existence. For, having contemplated the various sufferings of cyclic existence, we must generate aversion for them, not wishing to be reborn in any of these states. Next we should find out the causes of suffering. All suffering is caused by the afflictive emotions — such as ignorance, attachment, and so on — and the three types of actions — virtuous, non-virtuous, and immovable. Actions arise because of the afflictive emotions and shoot one into cyclic existence like an arrow from a bow. The afflictive emotions, in turn, are caused by misconceptions that arise from our distorted mental activities. Because afflictive emotions are the principal cause of suffering, we must remain constantly aware of the harmfulness of the misconceptions that cause them, for they project happiness upon misery and permanence upon impermanence.

Remember the ills of attachment to objects in general and to desirable objects such as wine in particular. Be mindful of the evils of hatred, which is mental turmoil over harm to yourself or those close to you, and of ignorance, which is confusion about the law of the cause and effect of actions and about emptiness. Keeping in mind the drawbacks of all these, abandon them.

The evils of these causes of suffering are referred to throughout Buddha's teachings. Buddha said in the *Sutra on Teachings That Are the Bases of Discipline ('dul ba lung gzhi'i mdo)*:

> Anyone who calls himself my disciple is not permitted even to dip a blade of grass in alcohol and taste it.

In another sutra a god asked a question in verse:

> Which are sharp weapons?
> Which virulent poison?
> Which a blazing fire?
> And which great darkness?

Buddha replied:

> Poisonous words are sharp weapons,
> Desire, the virulent poison,
> Hatred, a blazing fire,
> And ignorance, the great darkness.

It is also said in scripture:

> There is no swamp like desire
> And no harm like hatred,
> Nothing is more extensive than ignorance,
> There is no river like attachment.

Also contemplate the twelve-linked chain of dependent-arising as set forth in the *Questions of Gaganaganja Sutra (nam mkha' mdzod kyis zhus pa, gaganagañjapariprcchā)*:

> The way of profound dependent-arising is as fol-

lows: ignorance conditions actions; actions condition consciousness; consciousness conditions name and form; name and form condition the six senses; the six senses condition contact; contact conditions feelings; feelings condition attachment; attachment conditions grasping; grasping conditions existence; existence conditions birth; birth conditions aging and death, sorrow, lamentation, suffering, misery, anguish, unhappiness, and agitation. In this way there come forth only great masses of misery. The exalted wisdom of the Bodhisattvas has penetrated to what the causes and conditions are by which a living being is completely fettered by the afflictive emotions. This is called the way that all existence comes forth, dependent-arising.

How is dependent-arising reversed? By the cessation of ignorance, there is cessation of actions; by the cessation of actions, there is cessation of consciousness; by the cessation of consciousness, there is cessation of name and form; by the cessation of name and form, there is cessation of the six senses; by the cessation of the six senses, there is cessation of contact; by the cessation of contact, there is cessation of feelings; by the cessation of feelings, there is cessation of attachment; by the cessation of attachment, there is cessation of grasping; by the cessation of grasping, there is cessation of existence; by the cessation of existence, there is cessation of birth; by the cessation of birth, there is cessation of aging and death, sorrow, lamentation, suffering, misery, anguish, unhappiness, and agitation. Thus there is cessation of the great masses of misery. This is called the way of ceasing the process of dependent-arising. The exalted wisdom of the Bodhisattvas has penetrated to what the causes and conditions are by which a living being is purified. This is called penetrating to the profound way of the teaching. This is not the way of Hearers or Self-Enlightened Ones.

The next step is to understand the nature of the path to liberation. Dzong-ka-ba says in the *Foundation of All Excellence*:

> That pure thought [of renunciation] draws forth
> The deep heedfulness of mindfulness and
> introspection.
> Bless me to accomplish by this means the essence
> Of the individual vow, the root of the teaching.
> (v.6)

Once we have fully realized the perniciousness of cyclic existence and desire to escape from it, then, motivated by the desire for liberation, we should take the excellent vow of individual liberation (*so sor thar pa, pratimokṣa*), the root of the teaching. We must cultivate the great heedfulness that consists of mindfulness, introspection, self-reproach, shame, and cautiousness — mindfulness, which does not forget what is to be done or not done; introspection, which constantly examines body, speech, and mind and discriminates between right and wrong actions; self-reproach, which causes us to shrink from wrongdoing; shame, which causes us to shrink from censure of spiritual friends; and cautiousness, which causes us to fear the effects of wrong actions.

Through this heedfulness, we can attain the essence of pure ethics. Guard it more dearly than your life, for ethics is the source of the trainings in meditative stabilization and wisdom — the source of all excellence.

As long as we have desire and attachment, we will wander in cyclic existence, a consequence we should greatly fear. Thus, through renunciation we enter the right path for stopping cyclic existence. What framework is needed to stop cyclic existence? Generally we need a human life endowed with leisure and opportunity, and particularly it is excellent to have a vow of renunciation. The wise take pleasure in the practice of renunciation.

What path should we cultivate in order to stop cyclic existence? The highest practice of the holy ones is the eightfold path: right view, right thought, right speech, right conduct, right livelihood, right effort, right mindfulness, and right meditation. These are all included within the three exceptional trainings: exceptional ethics, exceptional meditative stabilization, and exceptional wisdom. We should learn these.

Buddha said in a sutra:

> Those who train in ethics
> Will necessarily have wisdom;
> Those who possess ethics
> Also have liberation.

Thus it is indicated that exceptional meditative stabilization, exceptional wisdom, and all other virtues arise in dependence on ethics. It is said throughout the sutras and their commentaries, "Ethics is the root of the teaching." Hence, we must train in ethics. The benefits of training in ethics are great, for ethics is the best happiness, the path to liberation, the field of complete knowledge, and the cause of Buddhahood.

In order to observe pure ethics we must learn to control our sense organs. Should we transgress any aspect of ethics, we must make effort at the methods for correcting our wrong. The source of all wrongdoing is the three mental poisons but the specific causes of transgressions are a lack of understanding, carelessness, disrespect, and uncontrolled afflictive emotions. After recognizing these, we must find and apply the antidotes to them — heedfulness and the seven jewels of the holy ones, i.e., faith, hearing, mindfulness, introspection, shame, self-reproach, and wisdom.

Finally, we reach the stages of the path for beings of great capacity. We can attain liberation by following the three exceptional trainings, but we will liberate only ourselves from the suffering of cyclic existence, fulfilling only the minor purposes of ourselves and others. Therefore, Buddha taught that one must finally enter the Mahayana path. There are two ways to enter this path: by first progressing through the practices of the small and then middling practitioners or by entering the Mahayana practices from the beginning. The latter is most excellent, for the Mahayana vehicle abounds in skillful means and is thus able to bring incalculable benefits and happiness to limitless sentient beings. Furthermore, this vehicle is endowed with the three most purposeful activities, which are attributes of the altruistic aspiration to enlightenment. That is, the altruistic aspiration acts as (1) the door for entering the Mahayana, (2) the basis of all Buddha's teachings, and (3) the method for quickly attaining Buddhahood.

There exists in each living being the potential for attaining Buddhahood, called the Buddha-essence (*de bzhin gshegs pa'i snying po, tathāgatagarbha*), the "legacy abiding within" (*rang bzhin gnas rigs, prakṛtiṣṭhagotra*). This Buddha-essence is the emptiness of the mind, which is untainted by any defilement, existing as pure from the very beginning even though in the midst of afflictive emotions. There is also the "developmental lineage" (*rgyas 'gyur gyi rigs, paripuṣṭagotra*), which is the cultivation of those mental states suitable for Buddhahood and is an attribute of beings of great capacity. Through this mental training one can produce the altruistic aspiration for highest enlightenment, the benefits of which are beyond measure. Once it has been produced, it is very important to train in the Bodhisattva-deeds.

Thus, the mental training for beings of great capacity consists of first producing the altruistic aspiration and then learning the Bodhisattva-deeds. Dzong-ka-ba says in the *Foundation of All Excellence*:

> Having seen that all beings, my former kind
> mothers,
> Have fallen like myself into the ocean of existence,

> May I practice the superior altruistic aspiration for
>   enlightenment,
> Which assumes the obligation to free all beings.
>   (v.7)

First develop equanimity toward all living beings. Then
think, "By the influence of actions and afflictive emotions,
I myself have fallen into the immeasurably deep ocean of
cyclic existence, and I am tortured ceaselessly by the croco-
diles of the three miseries. With my mind's eye I can see
that all living beings, who have been my infinitely kind
mother again and again, are also tortured by the misery of
cyclic existence. In return for their kindness, may all beings
meet with undefiled happiness. May they be free from all
misery. May I myself cause this to happen."

Thinking thus, we produce the high resolve to assume
the obligation to free all beings. Then to the extent of our
ability we must repeatedly develop the precious altruistic
aspiration to highest enlightenment, the root and vital force
of the Mahayana, thinking, "I will attain perfect Buddhahood in order to free all beings from suffering."

In order to generate the altruistic aspiration it is essential
to cultivate the four immeasurables: compassion, loving
kindness, joy, and equanimity. We must conceive of each
and every sentient being as our former mother, father,
sister, brother, or any other close person. Then we must
produce compassion desiring to free them from suffering,
loving kindness wishing that they have happiness, joy that
delights in their freedom from suffering and possession of
happiness, and equanimity that impartially wishes that all
beings have such enjoyment.

Next we must engage in the six perfections — giving,
ethics, patience, effort, concentration, and wisdom — and
the four means of assembling disciples — giving gifts to
the disciples, speaking kindly to them, acting for their
benefit, and acting in accordance with our own teachings.
Among the six perfections, concentration and wisdom are
most important. Concerning those two Dzong-ka-ba says in

the *Foundation of All Excellence*:

> By quieting attraction to wrong objects
> And properly analyzing the meaning of reality
> Bless me to quickly produce in myself
> The path of unified tranquillity (concentration) and
>   insight (wisdom). (v.9)

In conclusion Dzong-ka-ɓa says in the following verse:

> Once by practicing this general path I become its
>   vessel,
> Bless me to easily enter
> The great gateway of the fortunate ones,
> The Vajrayana, highest of all vehicles.

Notes

Introduction

1. Geshe Wangyal, *The Door of Liberation*, (New York: Lotsawa, 1978), pp. 94-95.

2. The Kalmucks were divided into three tribes. Those towards the center of Kalmuck country were members of either the Durbot or Tourgut tribes. Those towards the outside of Kalmuck country were members of the Buzawa tribe. The Buzawas tended to adopt more of the customs of their Russian neighbors, whereas the other two tribes reacted against such changes in their tradition. The monastery of philosophical studies which Geshe Wangyal, a Durbot, attended was located among the Durbots, who considered themselves the most learned with respect to the teaching. The second such monastery was located amongst the Tourguts.

3. This method of divination involves casting dice and then interpreting the numbers according to a text's explanation. A lama who is accurate is thought to possess some spiritual power.

4. Geshe Wangyal, *The Door of Liberation*, pp. 81-82.

5. *ibid*, pp. 102-103.

6. Oral teaching of Loseling Kensur Yeshe Tupden

given at the Tibetan Buddhist Learning Center's seminar on death and impermanence on April 19, 1985.

7. This relationship started when the Third Dalai Lama, Sonam Gyatso (*bsod nams rgya mtsho*, 1543-1588), became the lama of Altan Khan, leader of the Mongol nation. Altan Khan gave Sonam Gyatso the title "Dalai Lama", or "Lama who is an Ocean (of Wisdom)". The two previous incarnations of Sonam Gyatso received the title posthumously.

8. Mind transference is a practice whereby one can send one's consciousness to a pure realm of Buddhas and Bodhisattvas at the moment of death.

Chapter One

9. This chapter is an edited version of a section from Sum-ba-ken-bo's (*sum pa mkhan po*) History of Buddhism in India and Tibet, Wishfulfilling Jewel Tree (*dpag bsam ljon bzang*).

10. Buddha's twelve deeds are: (1) being born in Tushita paradise, (2) descending from Tushita, (3) entering the mother's womb, (4) being born, (5) displaying artistic skills, (6) enjoying life with his princesses, (7) renouncing worldly life and undertaking ascetic practices, (8) departing in order to attain enlightenment, (9) overcoming the hosts of devils, (10) attaining perfect enlightenment, (11) turning the wheel of the teaching, and (12) entering final nirvana.

11. The three natures (*rang bzhin gsum, trisvabhāva*) are imputations (*kun brtags, parikalpita*), dependent phenomena (*gzhan dbang, paratantra*), and thoroughly established phenomena (*yongs grub, pariniṣpanna*).

12. Female enlightened beings who assist others in their practice.

Chapter Two

13. This chapter is adapted from Den-dar-hla-ram-ba's (*bstan dar lha ram pa*) Words Proving That the Teacher is a Perfectly Right Being: A Jeweled Staircase Reaching the

Palace of Great Bliss (ston pa tshad ma'i skyes bur sgrub pa'i gtam bde chen khang bzang 'dzeg pa'i rin chen them skas).

14. The Tibetan is: tshad mar gyur pa 'gro la phan bshed pa/ ston pa bde gshegs skyob la phyag 'tshal te/

15. The Tibetan translation of the Sanskrit *arhat*, or *ari-han*, is *dgra bcom pa*. A literal English translation of this would be "One who has conquered (*han*) his [inner] enemy (*ari*), [selfishness]."

16. A Buddhist who has not attained liberation.

17. A proper example to support a reasoning is something that the opponent understands and accepts. Although desire is not a wholesome mental quality, it does increase without relying on renewed effort.

18. Based on this reasoning, Kay-drup-jay (*mkhas grub rje*) in his *Clearing Mental Darkness with Respect to the Seven Sections on Reasoning (rigs pa sde bdun yid kyi mun sel)* treats in detail the reasoning that proves the existence of former and future lives.

19. Dharmakirti explains this in the second chapter of his *Precise Commentary on (Dignaga's) "Compendium on Right Perception"*, the "Proof of Right Perception" (*tshad ma grub pa, pramāṇasiddhi*), starting with the line, "The proof begins with the cultivation of compassion," and continuing through the phrase, "One who is freed from attachment turns the mind from attachment."

20. Dharmakirti explains this in the second chapter of his *Precise Commentary* with the lines from "Having mercy in order to eradicate suffering," through to "Are explained as the causes of those two."

21. Dharmakirti explains this is the second chapter of his *Precise Commentary* with the lines from "The Sugata having the three causal qualities of abandonment" through to "One who knows that achieves."

22. Dharmakirti explains this in the same chapter as above with the lines from "The rescuer spoke the path he saw," through to "Therefore he is said to be a perfectly right being."

23. Dharmakirti also explains this in his second chapter, "Moreover the rescuer taught the four noble truths."

24. Dharmakirti explains this in his second chapter, from "From liberating he possesses that," through to "Because he has reached the level of no-more-to-learn."

25. Dharmakirti describes this in his second chapter, "As he attained the fulfillment of others' purposes, he is the teacher."

26. As Dharmakirti states in his second chapter, "From that [direct cognition of selflessness one can deduce] compassion."

27. This proof statement is an effect reason proving that Buddha is omniscient. It is the actual reasoning for proving the "omniscient one", or "one who became perfectly right" in Dignaga's salutation.

Chapter Three

28. This chapter is taken from Ḍen-ɓay-drön-may's (*btsan pa'i sgron me*) *Final Commentary of the Difficult Aspects of the Interpretable and the Definitive: The Quintessence of (Ḍzong-ka-ɓa's) Essence of the Good Explanations* (*drang nges rnam 'byed kyi dka' 'grel rtsom 'phro legs bshad snying po'i yang snying*).

29. The two Hearer sects are the Hearers (*nyan thos, śrāvaka*) and Self-Enlightened Ones (rang sangs rgyas, *pratyekabuddha*).

30. An affirming negation would be "the pot that has no water", and a non-affirming negative would be "the pot does not exist".

31. The tenets of the Consequence Middle Way School are considered throughout Tibet and Mongolia to be the most exact exprèssion of Buddha's teachings on emptiness and its relation to conventional objects.

Chapter Four

32. These eight are: gain and loss, fame and disgrace, praise and blame, and pleasure and pain.

33. *lam rim bsdus don*. See Geshe Wangyal, *Door of Liberation* (New York: Lotsawa, 1978), p. 241.

34. This chapter is Geshe Wangyal's translation of verses that he composed in Tibetan, based on the "stages of the path" teachings.

35. These three are desire, hatred, and ignorance.

36. Desire, hatred, ignorance, pride, and competitiveness.

Chapter Five

37. This chapter is an adaptation based on two works: Den-dar-hla-ram-ba's *Precious Good Vase That Fulfills Many Wishes: Speech That is Composed From the Method of Going for Refuge* (*skyabs su 'gro ba'i tshul las brtsams pa'i gtam 'dod dgu 'jo ba'i rin chen bum bzang*) and Den-bay-drön-may's *Lamp Illuminating the Good Path of Happiness and Benefit: Instructions on the Practice of Going for Refuge, the Entrance to the Teaching* (*bstan pa'i 'jug sgo skyabs 'gro'i khrid yig phan bde'i lam bzang gsal ba'i sgron me*).

38. These gods are still caught up in the world and have yet to attain liberation.

39. This is taught in detail in the *Door of Liberation*.

40. A representation of Buddha's body would be a Buddha image; of his speech, a book of the teaching; and of his mind, a memorial of enlightenment (*chos rten, stupa*).

41. Root lama: one's fundamental spiritual master, or *guru*.

42. past, present, and future.

43. According to the sutra method, it is not necessary to visualize purifying streams of nectar coming from the protectors; the rays of light alone give you blessings.

44. loving kindness, compassion, joy, and equanimity.

45. Sometimes the verse on equanimity is recited before the verse on loving-kindness; you may recite it in whichever order you prefer.

46. This is translated in the *Door of Liberation*, p. 116.

47. These prayers are also translated in the *Door of Li-*

beration.

48. The four rivers are explained either as the rivers of desire, existence, ignorance, and dogmatism, or as the rivers of birth, sickness, old age, and death.

Chapter Six

49. This chapter is freely adapted from Ba-drul Jik-may-chö-gi-wang-bo's (*dpal sprul 'jigs med chos kyi dbang po*) *Instructions on the Preliminaries to the Great Perfection Teaching Called "Heart Essence of Vast Openness"*, the *Sacred Word of Lama Gun-sang* (*rdzogs pa chen po klong chen snying tig gi sngon 'gro'i khrid yig kun bzang bla ma'i zhal lung*).

Chapter Seven

50. This chapter is taken from Dzong-ka-ba's *Great Exposition of the Stages of the Path.*

Chapter Eight

51. This chapter is an edited version of Den-bay-drön-may's *Entrance Way for the Supreme Vehicle: How to Meditate on the Two Minds of Enlightenment* (*byang chub kyi sems gnyis sgom tshul theg pa mchog gi 'jug ngogs*).

Chapter Nine

52. This chapter is an adaptation drawn from two works by Den-dar-hla-ram-ba: *A Particle of Nectar: A Refutation of Error Extracted from the Ocean of Good Explanation, a Presentation of the Lack of Being One or Many* (*gcig du bral gyi rnam gzhag legs bshad rgya mtsho la btus pa'i 'khrul spong bdud rtsi'i gzegs ma*) and *Precious Garland: A Commentary on the Meaning Focusing on the Difficult Points of* (*Dzong-ka-ba's*) *"Praise of Dependent — Arising"* (*rten 'brel bstod pa'i dka'i gnas las brtsam pa'i don 'grel rin chen phreng ba*). The following explanation accords with the view of the Middle Way Autonomy School (*dbu ma rang rgyud pa, svātantrika-mādhyamika*).

53. A correct mind (*blo gnod med*) is one not defiled by any superficial cause of error.

54. This work is translated in Geshe Wangyal's previous book, *Door of Liberation* (New York: Lotsawa, 1978), under the title *The Essence of Good Explanation, Praise to Munindra* (*thub pa'i dbang po'i bstod pa legs bshad snying po*).

Chapter Ten

55. This chapter is adapted from Gushri Gap-ju-sudhī's (*kuśri dka' bcu sudhī*) [also known as Gap-ju-ma-wa Lo-sang-tsay-pel (*dka' bcu smra ba blo bzang tshe 'phel*)] *Good Path of the Conqueror: An Explanation Combining the Precious Scriptures of the Conqueror and (Dzong-ka-ba's) "Opener of the Supreme Path"* (*rgyal ba'i gsung rab rin po che dang lam mchog sgo 'byed gnyis sbyar te bshad pa rgyal ba'i lam bzang*).

Index